Life:

In-an-Instant Moments

ISAIAH F. COBB

WESTBOW
PRESS®
A DIVISION OF THOMAS NELSON
& ZONDERVAN

WestBow Press books may be ordered through booksellers or by contacting:

WestBow Press
A Division of Thomas Nelson & Zondervan
1663 Liberty Drive
Bloomington, IN 47403
www.westbowpress.com
844-714-3454

ISBN: 978-1-6642-8926-0 (sc)
ISBN: 978-1-6642-8927-7 (hc)
ISBN: 978-1-6642-8928-4 (e)

Library of Congress Control Number: 2023900773

Print information available on the last page.

WestBow Press rev. date: 02/09/2023

CONTENTS

PREFACE

At some point in your life, you may have thought that your job, family, and everything else were doing wonderfully. On any given day, everything was in order and appeared to be under control. Remember these words: *appears* to be under control.

In an instant, however, your world starts to shatter like precious crystal under tons of solid steel.

What do you do in such a dark season of your life? Do you admit defeat, or do you stand your ground and fight? The answer is simple. You hold firm to your faith in God and fight. And if you do not have faith of that degree, get it quickly!

This book is a fraction of my life story. I hope you will be blessed and inspired by the words on these pages. My desire is to share these stories and testimonies as a witness for God to humankind for generations to come.

ACKNOWLEDGMENTS

I thank God for my creativity, instilled in me before conception by my parents. My desire is to glorify Him as I share my testimonies and stories, with love, with my fellow human beings. I am forever grateful; it is a joy to do so as a witness for others to believe and receive the Salvation of Jesus Christ. I would like to thank my dad and mom, Robert and Frankie; my wife, Yvonne; my mother-in-law, Esther; my stepson and his wife, Duane and Crystal; my daughters, Anna and Alena; and all my siblings, all of whom helped to shape and mold me into who I am today. I thank God for their support and inspiration as they encouraged me to write this book.

Furthermore, I'd like to thank my parents for raising my siblings and me in a Christian home. Our parents taught us about character so we would develop an enthusiastic respect for others. The lesson learned was how to respect others, no matter what color their skin may be. The joy I feel in my spirit for being obedient to the Spirit of God is personal to me. It is because of the relationship I have with Him. I love to praise, worship, and glorify God because of His grace and mercy to me and all humankind.

There are many more thanks to share on behalf of my family and others for their prayers, concerns, encouragement, and love. The beauty of this book is not who wrote it. Instead, it is the anointing given to me and my being obedient to write it to the glory of God.

CHAPTER 1

◆

Life: A Faith Builder

In 2015, changes at my job—I worked at a printing fulfillment distribution company—occurred like nothing I had ever seen. I was not fully prepared, nor did I have a desire, for the many changes that were at my doorstep.

January was one of the slow months of the year, and work could be unpredictable; some days we were busy, and others were terribly slow. The goal was to stay busy by cleaning and doing something productive.

In early February, I was called for jury duty in March for two weeks. It is an honor to serve one's local government in any capacity, and I thanked and praised my God for allowing me this opportunity. I eagerly awaited the day when I was to report and serve my local government in Columbus, Ohio.

It was a Monday, and I had to be at the courthouse by 8:30 a.m. This was a milestone in my life; serving as a juror for a period of two weeks was a learning experience I would not soon forget and would cherish for years to come. Different judges spoke each day to the jurors, asking and answering various questions to help us better understand the court system. The rigorous process that each court case went through to stay within the legal boundaries of justice amazed me.

As my two weeks of jury duty started to wind down, I knew I

would have to return to work soon. When I did, I heard astounding news—the company for which I had worked since August 20, 2000, was now for sale because of financial challenges. It was hard for a company to function without appropriate funds, and it was even harder for employees to stand without a solid foundation on a day-to-day basis. Still, I hoped for the best. My faith was still built on the solid foundation of my Lord and Savior, Jesus Christ. I knew in my spirit that, somehow, everything would be fine, and I praised God for my faith in Him.

In my career of almost forty years, I have learned that positions come and go, but my God will always be there, no matter what I face in life. Little did I know how true this would be before 2015 ended.

At work, I did my best to keep an open mind about the matter that was coming down the track at a locomotive's speed. I had questions about various matters at hand. Who were the new owners? Would there be changes for the senior employees? Would benefits change? Oh, so many questions with no truthful answers.

In early April 2015, some of my coworkers and I were trying to better understand what to do about this situation over which we had little to no control. It was a simple answer; we had to wait! It was a very emotional wait, even for the best of us. At times, there was some reassurance by Human Resources Personnel, but they had little effect on the matter. A large number of senior employees resigned from their positions. In a brief period, I saw six coworkers resign, one after the other; their combined experience was equivalent to one hundred years of service to the company. This loss appeared to be of little concern to the management team.

It came at a time of great surprises in my life; I was over fifty years old at that point. Often, I desired it to be different, but God was in control of the situation, and my trust was in Him and will be to the very end of life.

Those four months, from the beginning of the year through April, challenged my faith as the dark clouds swirled toward me. They clouded my mind and made it difficult to see. They were a storm filled with emotions and great pain, and I did not have a clue how close it was to reality. The company proceeded with business as usual, but it was far from being that.

The emotional impact from not knowing what to expect from day to day was taking a toll on my body, physically and mentally. I had to work overtime early in the mornings and had long workdays. The morale of my coworkers and me shifted in a southward direction each day. It became more difficult to endure the uncertainty at the workplace, but each day, I pressed on in Christ Jesus; my hope, faith, and trust for the present and future were in Him alone.

As May entered the arena, the birth of hope appeared in my mind a lot. Before I moved to Ohio, I had experienced something similar, and it had prepared me for such a season in my life. I share my testimony in the hope that my story will reach into the pain of others to give them hope for their future.

I reflected on the early spring of 1982, when I found myself without a job, just as I did in early spring of 2016. In 1982, I filled out volumes of applications in search of the job God had for me, hoping for a positive response, but nothing happened.

One day, I was lying in bed, talking to God about my situation. "I am without a job," I said. "I have no form of income, and I have almost depleted the funds in my checking account."

Of course, God knew about my situation, but I wanted to share it with Him as a reminder to myself. On a sunny spring morning, after I'd had the conversation with God, I was traveling on Gordon Highway in Augusta, Georgia. I glanced over my right shoulder and saw a business located in a valley-like setting. *How fitting*, I thought. *The valley is low and so am I.* As I was feeling my lowest, I heard a voice say, *Go to that place and apply for a job.*

I had driven beyond the road that led to that business, so I made a U-turn and headed back to that business to apply for a job. I headed home afterward. What followed is just like God; by the time I arrived home, the manager of that business had called and left a message with my mom. I was to call him as soon as possible. When I spoke with him, we scheduled an interview for the following day.

This story gets even better. I went to the interview, and it went well; the manager made me an offer. When I returned home around 3:00 p.m., another blessing was in place—another person had called and left a message for me. I called him back, and guess what? I now had two job offers to choose from. In an instant (fewer than three days), my life shifted from a negative to a positive blessing. I took the first offer.

I am in awe of how God took my situation and turned it around in an instant. My praise is to God now and forever.

Nobody knows what will take place in one's life on any given day, but God knows. For Mother's Day in May 2015, I did the usual things, such as trying to choose the most beautiful card for my sweet and loving mother. I also wanted to give her something just because of who she was. I blessed her with a monetary gift to spend on herself for all the love she had given from the very first day of my life; for that, I am forever grateful.

I tried to stay in touch with my mother every week so she would know how grateful and appreciative I was for her teaching and love each day. It helped to shape me and prepare me for life. That particular Mother's Day holds a special place in my heart because it was the last Mother's Day that I shared with her in this earthly life.

This is one reason to show love to your mother while she is alive. You may not agree completely on everything, and your views of various issues may not be the same, but you can rest assured that genuine love from the heart will overpower any opposition you may encounter in life. All Mother's Days can be beautiful when the love of family is there to surround their mother with their love, not for a day but for the rest of her life.

I welcomed June 2015 with open arms and a warm embrace, but that month was like a Niagara Falls of emotions for my family and me. In an instant, our lives changed forever. June started out great; there was love in celebrating our blessing with my mother, siblings, daughters, and others. But later that month, I encountered a pain that nobody could heal, except the Lord and Savior Jesus Christ.

As my and my daughter's birthdays approached, my faith

and emotions were bittersweet because they were put to test. We celebrated my birthday and Father's Day in mid-June by going out for dinner. We had an enjoyable time, and the food was delicious. After dinner, we returned home and enjoyed the company and blessing of family. Around 10:00 p.m., I turned in for the night— the rest of the family already was in bed or preparing to get there. Shortly afterward, I drifted into a deep sleep.

In an instant, my and my family's lives were changed forever when our home phone rang. Even though I was sleeping, I instantly was awakened by the ringing of the phone. I glanced at the clock on the dresser and saw it was past midnight.

At that hour of the night, I have learned it's usually sad or unwelcome news. I answered the phone, and the second I heard my sister's voice, I felt what she was about to say: "Mom has passed." It was only a short time after the end of my wonderful day of celebration with my family, which made it difficult to accept the news. In an instant, my world changed forever. It was like an out-of-control roller coaster, speeding down the tracks for the rest of my life. After I received the sad news, it was exceedingly difficult for me to return to sleep, so I talked to my wife about the phone call.

This I know: my mom was the sweetest woman I ever knew this side of heaven. I love and miss her dearly. The beauty of my mother's love is easy to explain in the following way: One winter when I was about nine years old, I contracted a cold or the flu and did not feel well. Mom rubbed some Vicks VapoRub on my chest and sent me to bed. Then, my mom did something that any loving mother would have done. No sooner had my head touched the pillow than my mom walked into the bedroom. She asked, "How are you feeling?"

I said, "I'm cold!"

Then she closed the top button on my pj's and tucked my bedcovers around me tightly. It left me with a warmed-blanket-like feeling. I feel the warmth of her love to this very day. That powerful feeling of my mother's love for me is something that I will never forget.

I am thankful always to my heavenly Father for my mother

because her love runs deep in my veins, and she shared it with me in so many ways. I will always remember that June for the sorrows and joy and a major change in my life. To that point, the year 2015 had challenged my faith to an emotional level. On one hand, it was the celebration of Father's Day and my birthday. On the other hand, it was the death and burial of my dear, loving mother.

After the funeral, I felt a void that I had never felt before, although my dad and oldest sister had passed few years earlier. The emptiness I felt from my mother's death, however, was different; her death had a greater impact on me emotionally. My mother gave birth to me by the grace of God, and that bond can never be replaced by anyone or anything in this world.

CHAPTER 2

◆

Life, Joy, and Peace

July dawned like a birth of a newborn baby—full of life and so much to give in love, living one day at a time. It had been about two weeks since Mom passed away. My sorrow rose like ocean waves. My emotions were like the tide, washing away the sorrow in each teardrop stain that spilled down my face. I knew healing from my mom's death would take some time and that God would see me through it until the end.

July was hot and full of summer fun. It so happened that our family reunion for my wife's side of the family took place in San Antonio, Texas. I was looking forward to vacation and rest time, which my body needed very badly. The planning for this vacation and reunion was part of the day-to-day activities by my wife, our daughters, and me.

Sometimes, you need to take a break from the hustle and bustle of the day and take a deep breath and exhale.

Finally, our day for the trip arrived, and the weather was spectacular for our long flight to San Antonio, Texas. The trip went smoothly, and we arrived on time to our destination. In Texas, the temperature was around 104 degrees and dry. But through it all, I enjoyed the time to get away from the stress of the day-to-day routine and to enjoy the moment with family and friends. We had a wonderful time and learned a lot about the history of The Alamo from our tour guide.

The beauty of life can be bittersweet at times. A few weeks earlier, the death of my mother caused painful emotions. I did not want to embrace that time in my life, but I knew I would eventually. My mom's memory and legacy helped us in raising our daughters. She taught me how to be the best parent to our daughters and to leave them with a legacy to share with the next generation, by the grace of God.

In August 2015, our family reunion ended, and I had to return to work. I would learn how to face my situations and issues as they came, but I knew God would help my family and me to face the painful days ahead. There would be days to come, with or without warning, when I would have to deal with my emotions.

When I returned to work, I found that many things had not changed. A representative from the corporate office came to the facility and shared some disappointing news with the employees. The announcement was made that a downsize of the facility was forthcoming, and some of the employees would lose their jobs.

I often saw an individual in a parking lot or on the side of a highway who asked for money, and I would think, *How did this person get in this predicament?* Now I had the answer: sometimes it is out of that person's hands. It's what life has dealt the individual with an instant blow that has brought him or her to that level of humbleness.

After the announcement, employees' faces were distorted and dismayed; their little hope had died. There were numerous questions but few answers. The company where I worked was sold less than a month later, after so many major changes had already been made. Several of the facilities had closed and positions were offered to employees to work at other facilities. The closings and employees leaving the company after many years did not cease. That was a sad day because of the new owners in this company's history. After all the work, sweat, time, and pain that had gone into building the company, the end result was in the hands of the new owners.

The transition of August into September was a welcome sight because hope was on the rise, but then hope was delayed because of various actions by the new owners, who revised the diverse benefits that once were in place to a more challenging one for the senior employees. It was a personal choice for everyone to decide for himself or herself to stay or resign from the company. There was a change of vacation time, paid holidays, working at various times, and hours of overtime. This delivered a stress overload to my body and my family time, but I decided to hang in there to see what the outcome would be.

I did well for a month, but something within my being shifted to the tension and emotional stress I felt in my body. I had arrived at work early one morning, between four o'clock and four thirty. I parked my car but sat inside for a moment, gathering my thoughts for the day and preparing my body and mind in prayer for the work of the day. After a few minutes, I was getting out of my car when I noticed I could barely move my body. My stress level was remarkably high—I had pain in various places and was sleep deprived. I knew that I needed rest. I finally was able to get out of the car. Once I got moving, it was easier to function and do my job.

September 2015 was challenging because of the overtime I worked, during the week and on weekends. This continued, on and off, until the day I turned in my resignation. The demands of working the overtime requested were greater than I could deliver on short notice. I did have a life *after* work. For these reasons, I was placed in the predicament of choosing between the two.

Many jobs put people in similar situations, but I asked myself this question: is this job good for me, or is it creating a stress level in my life that will be harmful to my health, as well as to my family? This avenue in my life had been shaken, and I felt the impact from it. I had to evaluate the matter and find a solution to the problem. Because it was a physical, spiritual, mental, emotional, financial, and social part of my life, I would not take it lightly.

On a refreshing autumn morning, I took a stand in faith and chose to do that which was best for me. In hindsight, I should have taken a leave of absence instead of resigning, but when it was done, my life changed in an instant for the better.

Stress is a mean and deadly force. It is like a cancer, a powerful and destructive enemy to the physical body, filled with pressure and tension that will make or break you, physically and mentally.

I refused to surrender to this enemy, however, because my faith in God was (and is) the greatest, most compelling spiritual power on which I could fix my mind, body, and spirit. There was a beauty behind the chaos during my storm, and it was not based on my own in-an-instant moments but on God's will for my life.

> We are troubled on every side, yet not distressed; We are perplexed, but not in despair; persecuted, but not forsaken; cast down, but not destroyed; For which because we faint not. But though our outward man may perish, yet the inward man is renewed day by day. (2 Corinthians 4:8–9, 16 KJV)

The following is an essay I wrote in 1999:

A Christian's Life

> Are you troubled on all sides and still have joy within? Are you distressed [or] perplexed but not in despair; persecuted but not destroyed? Welcome, my brothers and sisters, to the life of being a Christian. Are you lied to, mistreated, put to many tests? Hold your head high because [in] being a Christian, you will not settle for less, for in Christ Jesus, the power of God is still in control, and you are forever blessed. A Christian's life on this earth consists of these things. My brothers and sisters, keep your eyes on Jesus Christ because He is your highest aim!

After I gave my two weeks' notice, words spread quickly that I was resigning from my position of fifteen-plus years. Many coworkers sought me to confirm that the news was true.

The next two weeks were perplexing to me, but they confirmed I'd made the right decision in resigning. I was at peace with God and myself.

On October 21, 2015, a crisp autumn day, I finished my final eight hours with the company that had been a great part of my life, including my family and wedding, for more than fifteen years. I could not allow this milestone in such a great journey pass without giving praise and thanks to my God. All the days when I reported to work, He gave me the strength, wisdom, courage, and knowledge to serve my position with integrity. Even when I was mistreated, I knew my work displayed integrity before others. My work was not just for that company and humans but for God because of my beliefs and faith in Him. This milestone in my life changed me, giving me greater faith and focus on the Savior, Jesus Christ.

CHAPTER 3

❖

There Is a Reason for Each Season

By the end of October 2015, I knew that I needed to get busy in finding another job. I had learned that God will always provide for His children, so I continued to trust Him. For the next two weeks, I received some much-needed rest for my body, mind, and soul. The end results were better sleep and more alertness, and my stress level lowered to a more endurable level.

My search for a new job intensified because a new position was on my path, with blessings for this season in my life. I applied for a position at a retail store but did not get a job offer, so I pressed on.

A few months later, I applied for another job. By that time, the job market had shifted to the technology of the twenty-first century, and I needed to use an electronic version of the application. It was easy for me to use the computer, and I uploaded my résumé and cover letters on various websites. I praised God for giving me a desire to learn the new technology. I applied for a position with a well-known retail company, and a few days later, I received a phone call to come for an interview, which led to a job offer. God had placed me in a new position, which then enhanced my résumé with new skills and experiences.

My faith rested in God, day after day. The new position was only a seasonal job, and I later learned that I was the first to hold that position. I was blessed to have worked that position for eight weeks; I learned and shared a lot with people.

My praise moment goes to God. He will supply all my needs, according to His plans and purpose for my life. I am grateful for this opportunity to share my story, testimony, and encouraging words, to be a blessing to others.

Anyone's life can change in an instant. My most important focus at that stage of my life was to know that whenever my life changed, I knew *whose* I was and *who* I was. The beauty I felt was electrifying. My colossal joy was knowing that the answer to my situation was in God's hands.

I believe whenever you put God first in your life, things will happen to you that you cannot explain. Instead, you can only share the testimony for the present and the future generation to come. Because of the death of my mother and uncle, who was the last of my mom's siblings, along with my resignation from my job and all the other emotional things that took place, the end of 2015 was bittersweet. I know the true meaning of the phrase *in-an-instant moments*.

After I finished my seasonal position in December 2015, I decided to take a moment to exhale and get some much-needed rest. The holidays were busy and demanded my time and focus because of the various gifts I wanted to purchase for my family. It was only by God's grace and mercy that I had been able to endure the year 2015. The new year 2016 was just around the corner. I knew that my breakthrough was on the way, like a locomotive racing down the track to reach its destination.

Whenever I see people on the side of the road with signs asking for money, I think it could be, at this stage in their lives, that they have had challenging times that have overshadowed their paths. And now, each one is trying to find his or her way home. In the streets they wander, trying to live day by day, hoping a breakthrough will come after the loss of a job from downsizing, the death of a spouse, or substance abuse has delivered a major blow.

In an instant, nobody truly knows what the future holds, but today and every day, I know who holds the future. My faith survives. It is in the Lord and Savior, Jesus Christ, who keeps me alive.

In 2016, I gave sincere praise to God that I'd made it, along with others, to that Happy New Year. Yet as I thought of the emotional aspect of 2015, I was reminded of the pain and emotions that swelled within me from time to time. I would not forget that I had endured these challenges, by God's grace and mercy.

In January 2016, I put my job search into action once again. A month earlier, I had applied for a position with the state of Ohio as an intermittent clerk and was told to expect a call sometime in January. By the middle of January, I had not yet received a call, but my faith in God held strong because of my belief in His Word:

> But my God will supply all your need according to his
> riches in glory by Christ Jesus. (Philippians 4:19 KJV)

My assurance would come when I had sustained the test that I was given for this season in my life. It was in my spirit that God knew my desire to endure all tests until life ends on this earth.

CHAPTER 4

◆

A Winter Blast Will Not Last

January 2016 was cold and gray on the outside and sometimes on the inside as well. The days of winter changed in an instant in the state of Ohio. The morning could start with sunshine and before half the day was gone, it could turn to snow, sleet, rain, ice, or all of the above.

When you have the guidance of the Holy Spirit, you have a Comforter who will never leave you.

That morning, I felt the Comforter (Holy Spirit) encouraging me to write during my storm. It was a witness that can encourage others as they go through their storms in life.

On any typical morning in the month of January 2016, I filled out application after application and sent several résumés online to various companies and businesses, seeking a position in the printing, graphics, or technology field. The responses I received were the same: *Thank you for applying to our business—* or something of that nature. It was not what I wanted to see in my search for a job, but each day and week in prayer, I pressed on in my search for that position that I knew God had for me. And when my faith stayed anchored to the Rock of Salvation in Jesus Christ, victory was mine.

February 2016 arrived like ocean waves drifting ashore in slow motion. The path before and after lets me know that God was still in control. I might not get my request answered in my timetable, but the answer would come, in God's time. In an instant, the end results caused my life to change for the better.

Around the second Friday in February, I was on the sofa, watching TV, when the phone rang. My wife answered and then called me to the phone.

The caller asked me a profound question that was music to my ears: "Are you still interested in the intermittent clerk position?"

"Yes!" I said immediately.

The caller offered me the job and told me when to report for work.

I gave God praise for giving me that position when I needed it most. In an instant, my life shifted to the real reason to give thanks in that new season—praise and being a witness for God.

In March 2016, I reported to work for the state of Ohio. I could not put into words the joy and happiness within me. But now, I can express it as a witness for others to see and know that God is faithful. Please remember this: no matter how dark your situation may seem, it will not last forever. When you walk in faith with Jesus Christ, everything will be all right.

My new position was a blessing. It offered good pay, easy work, and great people to work with. All good things must end, however, and because this was another seasonal position, my last day at work was May 18, 2016.

I once again had to seek a position that God had for me. I asked God for another breakthrough by providing me with the right job, in the name of Jesus Christ. He had done it in the past, and I knew that He would do it again. My faith in God was stronger than before because I knew what He had done in the past and present and could do in the future. He was not different because He changes not.

Early one morning, around 3:25, I was up, praying and asking God to do the impossible (from humankind's perspective). In contrast, in my spirit, I had the faith that He would do it in a powerful way, as witness for generations to come. I sent numerous résumés and applications to several businesses. My breakthrough was on my path of blessings for me to receive. It was a witness for others to see the power of a loving God. I said, "Thank you, God, for all of things you're doing as I write my story as a testimony." I knew that it would take only a fraction of a second, and this could become another in-an-instant moment once again.

By the following Friday, I put my search for a new job into overdrive. As I drove to various places searching for work, I saw many notices indicating that they accepted only online applications. I thought, *The search for a job has changed over the years. It once was face-to-face contact to apply for a position. This is now a twenty-first-century search.*

◆ ◆ ◆

In this technological age, the dependence on the computer is always in focus and forever changing. There is much to learn that can make one's life better, but does it call into question the way we socialize with our fellow human beings? Does it build character in an individual, so we know with whom we are working with on any given day? Whenever we lose our way in life, we lose our desire to fulfill our purposes in life. The gift of technology is a powerful force to contend with, but it is not the Almighty Force (Holy Spirit), which the soul of humankind needs.

CHAPTER 5

◆

Life Reflection for Strength

June 2016 was the month in which my life changed in an instant. It was my mother's and my uncle's deaths caused some profound emotions to rise within me, like the sunshine reaching for the blue sky. On Friday, May 27, 2016, I had a moment in which I sobbed. I do not know what brought on the emotional moment, but I knew I needed to cry. It was for my mother and my uncle's behalf as well. They were gone, never to return in this earth.

◆ ◆ ◆

I often think about the hardship and pain that come with each in-an-instant moment in our lives. In contrast, there are happy moments to remember as well. I believe the balance for life lies in the pages of the Holy Bible. This book is the book above all books. It gives us many profound stories of the happy and sad moments from the many generations of humankind that have gone before us.

◆ ◆ ◆

On that day, my search for work was still on my life path. By the will of God, I would serve in that purpose that He had for me. I did not know why I was writing a book at that stage in my life, but I knew that my story needed to be told, not only for the present season but for future generations. My story would become their encouragement for their seasons in which they lived.

During that week, my limbs of faith were tossed about but not uprooted. A few days later, I received an e-mail in response to a job application I'd sent in May 2016. The HR person and I talked for a moment, and she explained the position. The conversation ended on a positive note, and she said she would check with the production manager to see what he thought about my qualifications for the advertised position.

The most bizarre thing happened after the phone call; our internet service and phone line went dead. I had no way to respond to e-mail. I was able to contact the phone company from my cell phone, and they tried to resolve the issue, but nothing came of it. The end result was an appointment for a service call to solve the problem. I thought, *of all the days for our phone service to go dead, why did it choose this day?*

I had learned that when things did not go according to plan, my faith in God increased to another level. It lets me know that the matter was in God's hands, and He was in control. My search for a job was put on hold. The redirecting was God's plan for my purpose in life, to be filled for His glory at that season in my life. It was another in-an-instant moment to live through, with faith in God.

As the weekend approached, my in-an-instant moments kept my faith in perspective. These moments changed my life forever.

In 2004, I was heading home and feeling good after a full day of work. It was raining, and suddenly, the traffic came to a complete stop. After a few minutes of being idle, I tried to see what the situation was, but there were so many vehicles that I could not see very far in front of me. As I continued to wait in traffic, I suddenly saw, in my peripheral vision, a car coming at a high rate of speed in the rain on a very wet road. In an instant, the driver lost control, and his car skidded off the highway and headed directly toward my vehicle at a dangerous rate of speed. As I stared at what was happening, I was speechless. I couldn't move my vehicle due to the stopped traffic in front, behind, and beside my vehicle.

One thing I learned from growing up in a Christian home (I thank God for my mother and father) was to pray every day because nobody knows what the future holds. As the driver and his vehicle continued to slide in my direction, another in-an-instant moment leaped into action. It was by the grace and power of God almighty that turned things around. In a fraction of second, that out-of-control car stopped sliding. It was if it had encountered an unseen force field, and it turned back in the direction in which it had started. Hallelujah—a glorious praise to my God for His mercy and grace in that moment when I needed Him the most. I could only imagine that when I needed His angels of protection, they were there for me in a crisis.

Believe this, my brother and sister: we all have a purpose in this life, and, by the grace of God, we need to serve in it to His glory.

The traffic proceeded, and I was able to head home on a glorious evening, driving safely in the loving arms of Jesus Christ.

CHAPTER 6

◆

When Hope Appears to Be on Vacation

In June 2016, my search for a job was still in the forefront. I continued to say, "It is all about God's timing, not my timetable. Although my faith is evaluated, I will take a stand and continue to give some valuable time to this matter. I will hold my faith close to my heart until my prayers are answered and even closer after my prayers have been answered."

In-an-instant moments can come at a moment's notice, and there's nothing you and I can do to change that.

As I reflected on my life, I was reminded about another in-an-instant moment that took place in my life when I thought that everything was great and that I was in control. One hot summer Sunday morning in the red-clay hills of Georgia, one of my sisters and I were on our way to church. That morning was bright and clear; not a cloud could be seen.

We drove through a small town called Keysville, and as we were heading out of town, about to cross a bridge, I heard a voice say, "Buckle up!" We had not buckled our seatbelts, as it was not the law for driver and passenger to be buckled at that time. As I continued to drive, I almost asked my sister if she'd heard the voice, but I did not say a word.

There was very little traffic that morning, but within a mile, we approached a hill, and as I drove over the hill, we saw that a pickup truck was in front of us. I trailed this vehicle for about a mile when, suddenly, the driver did something very careless. Without signaling, he slowed down to turn off onto a county road. In an instant, a thought went through my mind: *Good, he is turning off this road.* But just as the thought entered my mind, this driver made a U-turn back onto the road, into the lane in which we were traveling.

My sister and I knew what was to come next—a terrible accident! I tried to avoid a direct hit to the front of my car by gradually turning the steering wheel to my left, but we collided into each other. The impact of our vehicles seemed to be in slow motion. My sister hit the windshield and sustained a cut to her forehead. I suffered a broken wrist from the inflating of the air bag. The driver of the pickup was unharmed. Oh, how life can change in an instant, right before one's eyes.

The impact of most in-an-instant moments can be overwhelming at times. After the accident, we were transported to the hospital. After the doctor examined us, he confirmed that my wrist was broken, and my sister's forehead was cut but did not require stitches. However, me returning to work was not on the menu, even though I wanted it to be. It was eight weeks, with half of my left arm in a cast, before I was able to return to work.

The heat from Georgia's summer sun was painful and hard to bear most days. As I reflected on that moment, I saw that it was preparing me for the opportunity to be a witness to others about the love of God in a time of need. My faith at that time continued to grow. When all is said and done, God gets the glory. He provided for me during that difficult moment in my life. God had already prepared me for such a season as that.

We may think we made it on our own strength in life, but in reality, we did not. If God removed His hand from our pathways, we would fall on our faces and not be able to get up. In order for people to know this, they have to be saved, but there are people who still need to learn this. There is a price to learning it; the price might be sleepless nights. For me, it was the testing of my faith, love, and selflessness by sharing my in-an-instant moments to the glory of God, as a witness to others.

I believe life has brought me to this moment to encourage the broken-hearted people of all ages. The most important thing you can do for your fellow human beings is to love them for who they are. They, too, have a purpose in life to fulfill to the glory of God. We all have a time to fulfill our purposes. I am incredibly grateful for this opportunity to share these words and to fulfill my purpose and be at peace with God and myself. I love to encourage the hearts of humankind as we journey across this earth.

In June 2016, I remembered two great sorrows from a year earlier. I had been reflecting a lot on the deaths of my mother and my uncle; they were last of their generation. They were gone but not forgotten for their contribution to humankind. My mother was special because she cared for her family and others. Many people saw that in her when they got the chance to know her.

She showed it in the preparation of meals. She used care and love in preparing the food—the right ingredients, baking, cooking, and tasting the foods, followed by the sweat, pain, and heat. She also made clothes and quilts whenever she got the chance to sew on her vintage sewing machine.

My uncle drove north from Savannah, Georgia, to my parents' home to visit his sister, nieces, and nephews. The love of family and sweet memories will never die when there are generations to follow. When it is shared, it becomes an ancestor's conduit as a witness, wrapped in the love and grace of God. These are the in-an-instant moments to hold dear, hoping and believing they will never die.

I praise you, my God, for such moments as these. Dear God, help me to leave such memories for my family as a legacy to share with their children and families.

During my job search that June, there were days when I got a response by phone or e-mail to set up an interview. One time, by e-mail, without speaking to a human being, I was able to set up an interview with a recruiter. Oh, how searching for jobs had changed due to the technology age and the changing ways that we socialized with one another.

How well do we know our neighbors? When we do not socialize face-to-face, does it create a mental picture and character about this person? Do we feel comfortable being around them? If we are communicating like this now, just imagine, what will it be like (God's willing) fifteen to twenty years from now?

One day, I received a voice message, asking me to call them. It was regarding a position for which I applied, but I hadn't heard anything until that moment. Nevertheless, because of my faith and whose and who I am, I pressed on. For me to receive what God has for me, it must be in His timing—and His alone.

In life, there are countless in-an-instant moments. I will share more of them to bless you and to be a witness for God and share what He does when we put our faith and trust in Him. It was in early spring, May 2010, and one of my nieces was graduating from high school in Augusta, Georgia. I had received an invitation to share in her celebration and accomplishments, and I was looking forward to it.

As her graduation day approached, I made a reservation to rent a vehicle for the trip to Augusta. Early on Friday morning, the day before the ceremony, I started my trip. In all my traveling across this beautiful land over the years, I have come to understand of the danger that is all around us each day. I have made it a traveling ritual to pray with my family and others before getting on the road to travel. On that Friday morning, I prayed the following prayer, titled "The Four B's Prayer" (go *before*, *beside*, *behind*, and *beneath*):

First, God will You go before me to keep the danger clear from my path as I travel. Second, God, will You go beside me to keep the danger from entering on the right or left side of me as I go. Third, God, will You go behind me to keep the other drivers, as well as me, from rear-ending other vehicles. Fourth, God, will You go beneath me to keep the roads and bridges (above and below) intact to take me safely to my destination, in Jesus Christ's name, amen.

In faith as a witness, God has been faithful to my request over the years. I am grateful to Him for doing so.

After praying on that Friday morning, I started my trip to Augusta. The weather was rainy and overcast. The traffic was mild because most people were at work or in school. The landscape on my drive to Georgia was scenic because of the various mountains, farms, and bridges. I praised God for all creations in life and for being able to see and learn about the various states and their history.

After being on the road about five hours, I stopped for gas, got something to eat, and made a restroom break. Shortly afterward, I was back on the road again, heading to Georgia. The remainder of my trip was easy driving because of the low traffic volume. I inhaled at that moment when I was taken from a fast-paced city setting to a much slower pace, a country setting, my kind of living. That was the reason I loved to travel across this great land.

Once I crossed the Georgia state line around 3:00 p.m., I stopped at a rest stop. In my mind, I thanked God for keeping me alive and safe as I drove south to my home state to be with my family. After arriving at one of my sisters' homes, I spent some time catching up on family news. Overall, it was simply good to be home! The old saying, "There is no place like home," held true for me.

On Saturday, I went to my niece's graduation. It was a beautiful ceremony and celebration of all the demanding work she put in over the years. Later that day, we had dinner with more members of the family at a nice restaurant in Martinez, Georgia. The company was great, and the food and service were good. After dinner, I returned to my sister's home, and we spent some more time catching up on old news. Shortly afterward, I went to bed; I had to leave early the following morning—before daylight—to return to Ohio.

Due to such long drive from Ohio to Georgia, my sleep was overly sweet, and I very much appreciated the rest. Around 4:30 on Sunday morning, I got dressed and told my sister goodbye. I thanked her for the lodging and company.

This is where my "Four B's Prayer" became a major reality in my life. I had only traveled few miles on that dark Sunday morning when, in an instant, a deer was standing on the right shoulder of the highway. I thanked God for His grace and mercy, as He showed it to me. In my prayer, I had asked God to go before, beside, behind, and beneath. The miraculous aspect of this matter was that the deer just stood there, and not once did the deer looked toward my vehicle's headlights. Also, the deer did not run across the interstate to the other side.

I understand deer; I used to hunt them for food. In a split second, they can run quickly across the road in front of you without any warning. But this deer just stood there and did not cross the road. I praised God for answering my prayer by keeping me safe as I traveled and visited family. To this day, I do not have an answer for that deer's behavior, except that God was totally in control on that Sunday morning.

CHAPTER 7

◆

Live Life and Celebrate It

On Father's Day, June 2016, my emotions remained very calm throughout the day. I would always remember the death of my mother and uncle around that time of the year. They were gone but not forgotten.

My job situation had not improved. I applied for many positions but received little feedback. I knew it only would take one in-an-instant moment for my life to be totally renewed, like the sunrise of a new day. My search for another job, however, was prolonged. My perception of life on earth was viewed through a new dimensional lens to learn and grow in my faith.

To men, women, boys, and girls, I have empathy for your pain. I can relate to how you may feel in your life situation if it is similar to mine. If you find yourself searching for or without a job, do not give up the search. When you have challenging moments, do not cease praying. If you're feeling low and cannot express yourself, press on, my friend. God knows what best for you. Life has many learning seasons. Those seasons may be painful, joyful, long, short, positive, and negative. But the key take-away from it all is to use it for a *learning foundation* to grow in your faith walk.

Only God knew how much I was expected to endure as I trusted in Him daily. My emotions took me to a low valley. It made me feel less of a human being, with no relief to embrace for strength to get through each day. The enemy tried to put doubts in my mind to make me question my faith. But with discernment from the Holy Spirit, I continued to stand on God's amazing grace. How did I know this? I had been at this level in my life before, and God changed everything in an instant. He provided me with a job at which I was able to work for over eleven years. My praise shout (hallelujah) went to my God of prevision and of my provision every day.

There may have been times in life when you said, "I am trusting in God!" But were you really trusting God? When the storms of life entered your world of comfort and peace and turned everything upside down, did you still trust God? Or did you trust in money and material things? What would you do if those things and money vanished in an instant? Would you take the high road instead of the low road? If your life was flipped inside out, what would you do? The answer is yours to choose. Choose it wisely!

Later, when I applied for assistance, the agency put me under the microscope. Why had I left my job? Even with such scrutiny from the agency, I applied for the position because I knew that I was 85–95% competent to do the job. Yet it was given to another candidate. I was told that seven questions would be asked, and the candidate with the highest score would get the job. My question was, "On what criteria was the grading process based?"

As another example, a position for which I applied was intercepted by a coworker. She handed the information to a friend of another coworker, informing him to apply for the position that was posted. The end result was that the person with the lesser seniority received the position. At that time, I felt like God was nowhere around. Did I stay anchored in my faith and continue to trust Him, or did I give up the fight? I maintained my faith in Him.

These are just a fraction of the challenges I faced to grow in my faith walk with Christ Jesus. If you had asked me how I felt while I was going through the various challenges, my answer would have been different. Today, I can say that those challenges increased my faith.

CHAPTER 8

◆

Faith to Endure Life

My in-an-instant moments increased my faith in Christ Jesus to a greater level. The most unorthodox things came at me in a bizarre way. I applied for a position, for example, and received a call for an interview, but the interviewer tried to interview me for a different position and ended the interview abruptly.

In another bizarre interview episode, after I was interviewed, I waited for three weeks without a follow-up response from the interviewer. I finally sent an e-mail, inquiring about the position. The response was not what I'd hoped for; the position had been given to another candidate. I learned this only after I inquired about the position.

From a dreamer's perspective, I say that the power of dreams allows the reality to reach its fruition. It can be an experience to increase one's faith. Sometimes, it means disappointment, such as not getting that ideal car, job, or house. From a tiny grain, such as a mustard seed, by faith, it becomes a plant or tree. The true evidence is the result birthed into the lives of the people to become better individuals. It will be a witness to all, every day and every way, in Christ, Jesus.

To be Christians, we need endurance (faith and the Holy Ghost, our Comforter) to go through various seasons in life. It can be stormy, rainy, gray, cold, or sunny; we can experience pain, suffering, disappointment, and sorrow. In contrast, a soft, gentle, warm breeze filled with peace internally can put our minds at ease. These storms will keep coming throughout the many seasons in our lives. But when we press on, we can get through the storms of life.

I wrote the following poem about striving and having determination to survive:

The Red Rose of Winter

There, beneath the dead of winter, lives a red rose
Much courage and determination within as it grows and grows
The ice that fell last night could not kill it with all its might
It seems appropriate to name it the Red Rose of Winter
Because it is quiet, cold, and gray on an icy winter night. [one's
      storms in life]
The rain from yesterday came and fell gently without much
      sunlight
It created tons of ice just over night, but this red rose kept its
      inward might

The temperature reached below zero
That was chilly, cold, and freezing
It created problems so great
Only God truly knows the true reason
A rose will live or soon its life will reach a final season

Now the ice, snow, and wind of winter have started to increase
And the ability to see life (for this rose), short or long term, has
      now decreased.
Yet, in faith, the desire is vital for this red rose to press on and live
Like yourself, because of the power (the Holy Ghost) only the
      Lord and Savior can give

31

Today, you can visualize yourself as a true red rose in the dead
of winter
The evidence of winter, snow and ice, has faded away
Leaving behind profound riches for a new spring day
The red rose of winter emerged (the contrast is like oneself,
from a life of sin)
Itself from the winter chill, by embracing the ultimate destination
in eternity to flourish and live.
Today, in Jesus Christ, you can be like the red rose of winter's past
Where only in eternity, you will forever last

CHAPTER 9

◆◆

God Is Real—He Makes a Way

In-an-instant moments can happen at any time or place. One of my moments happened in Georgia. It was early spring in 1997, and I'd made plans to drive to Atlanta for three days to an indoor camp revival. I left early on a Thursday morning. The drive was very pleasant, and the traffic was light. As I exited the interstate, my car stopped at the first red light, and the engine would not start. I knew something about vehicles and saw no reason why it should not start, but my car did not do a thing. The engine turned over but would not start.

After three attempts, I stepped out of my car to raise the hood to see if I could diagnose the problem. As I did so, I noticed an elderly lady sitting on a park bench. Before anyone else could help, she did so first. Of course, I was thankful to her for doing so. Shortly afterward, an attendant from the service station across the street came to my rescue. He suggested that the problem was with the gas pump. He offered to fix it and even said that if it was not the pump, I would not have to pay for his services.

It so happened that I needed a hotel for the next three nights. Across the street, within walking distance, was a hotel. Oh, how I thanked my God. He was my prevision for my provision (able to see and provide) in my time of need. After talking to the service station attendant, I retrieved my luggage and personal things from the car and walked across the street to check into the hotel.

After I settled into my room, I called one of the sisters who was a member at the church that I was to attend for the next few days. We had met few months earlier at a church service in another city. That was when I'd told her that I would come to the indoor camp service at her church. I told her what had happened to my car, and she was a major help in my situation. Later that evening, this sister came to take me to church.

I explained to the church members about my situation with my car, and they offered their assistance and prayers. I had a joyful time in service on that evening. This sister drove me back to the hotel. We talked and shortly afterward, we said good night. Once inside the hotel, I called two of my (sibling) sisters to let them know I had made it safely to Atlanta, but my car had died on arrival. I also let them know I was getting help from a sister from the church.

Since my day had started incredibly early, I felt overwhelmed with tiredness. I visualized the comfort of the bed, and not too long afterward, I was in bed.

Early the next morning, after breakfast, I returned to the service station to learn the diagnosis on my car, but the attendant had not decided on a solution to the problem.

Once again, the same faithful sister drove me to the church for the morning service. It was such a blessing to be a part of the service. The preaching, singing, teaching, praying, and testimonies were inspiring and encouraging to me, just when I needed it most. The evening service was a blessing; my brothers and sisters prayed and encouraged me that my car would be repaired. Then I could return home after the indoor revival service. Little did I know that my tiny grain of faith, the size of a mustard seed, was put into action by the grace of God.

After returning to the hotel on the second night, I went to bed shortly afterward, and it was revealed to me in a dream where to take my car to get it fixed. I got out of bed to search the phone book for the dealership name from my dream. I found it, wrote the name on a piece of paper, and went back to sleep. *God is so good*, I thought.

The most miraculous thing took place early the next day. The sister who was helping me called to say that her mom had a message for me. "She says that the problem is quite simple." The sister (from the church) said, "and it will be fixed."

I called the dealership and was told to bring the car in—but he was not sure he could get to it before they closed—it was a Saturday, and they were closing early.

I quickly retrieved my car from the service station. I did not have to pay anything, just as the attendant had said. I thanked him and started my drive to the dealership that was listed in the phone book. As I was driving, my car started to pop and sputter with loud sounds. Shortly afterward, it died. I had to walk to a pay phone and call for a tow to the dealership. After arriving there, I went to the service desk and was given not-so-pleasant news. First, the manager said they were closing at noon. And second, they did not have a rental vehicle.

The service manager then asked me the year of my car and its mileage. I gave him the answers, and he did something that left me in awe. He asked a mechanic to tell the tow truck driver to drop my car in the shop. This was the same man who had told me that he might not be able to work on my car that morning. But God!

Shortly afterward, a mechanic checked to see if he could pinpoint the problem. I stood at a distance to observe him as he worked on my car. After few minutes, he told the service manager that he had diagnosed the problem. A burned coil wire had caused the issue to my car, and he said he could fix it in a few minutes. After hearing the good news, I went to the customers' lounge and waited until my car was repaired. No sooner had I taken my seat to watch some TV than I heard my name called, followed by, "Your car is ready."

I hurried to the service floor and asked the service manager, "What is the cost?" I hoped I wouldn't hear words that were unwelcome to my ears. Instead, the manager again asked me a question, "What year is your car? What's the mileage?" After I answered, he said, "I'll do the repair under warranty."

In my spirit, a happy praise thought ensued that the service was covered under warranty. I praised my God.

The love He shows and the answer to His children's prayers are blessings and hope to stand in faith every day.

After the paperwork was processed, the service manager handed me my keys, and soon I was on my way back to the hotel. On the way there, my emotions got the best of me. A flow of tears ran down my face because of the way God had showed Himself faithful in my situation. On that Saturday morning, it was a dream (being obedient) and then the confirmation by the sister who assisted me in my crisis, which made it a reality. My car was fixed with no charge to me. Oh, I loved to serve my almighty God!

At the hotel, I could not wait to call and share the wonderful new to the sister who had stood by me through my ordeal. I shared my testimony as a witness for God to the pastor, and my sisters and brothers at church. When I returned home, I also shared it with my family.

I would like to share words of encouragement with you. If you find yourself in a situation similar to mine, and you feel that nobody cares, just acknowledge God and ask Him to help you. Have faith and believe that He will do it.

CHAPTER 10

◆◆

The Strength to Go On

In the third week in June 2016, I sought a full-time position. The wait was difficult to embrace at times. Sometimes, I felt like nobody had a clue about what I was going through, but that was not the case because Jesus Christ already knew. On any given day, I needed to be renewed in hope, faith, and trust in God. I often asked myself, *How can I get there from where I am standing?* It could not be done under my own strength, but only through the power of God, the Father; Jesus Christ, the Son; and the Holy Spirit, all in one.

There were days when I felt like my faith was on empty. A rechargeable connection was nowhere for my eyes to see. But in faith, I could visualize the difference, just when I thought I could not go on. I received a newness of strength on my faith journey to reach my eternal destination with Jesus Christ.

Many times, I've found myself thinking, *How did I get to this level in life that questions my faith and trust in God?* The enemy has a way to bring one's faith into question. Here are few of the questions the enemy poses: If God knows how you feel, why doesn't He do something about it? If God sees and knows your need, physically, why hasn't He responded to your situation? If God sees you walking in faith in Him, why doesn't He make the faith walk easier to walk? As my pastor, Bishop T. J. Clarke (First Church of God, Columbus, Ohio), would say, "I'm so glad you asked."

In this world, the weapon of the enemy is to deal with our minds, emotions, and hearts. Whenever we allow the enemy to take control of our minds, the emotions and heart will follow whatever we desire to do with our bodies. To paraphrase Romans 12:1–2, our bodies are not our own; they belong to God, the Creator of life. (The soul already belongs to God. Genesis 2:7 tells us that He breathed life into man's body, and man became a living soul.) Each day, we need to give what is due to the Creator of life, for He is over all of us.

Our bodies are the greatest gift to give to Him. This is why we need to ask God to renew our minds daily to live the life He has created for us to live. Our emotions and hearts are hard to control under our own strength. We need the spiritual power (Holy Ghost) from God more than our physical power to live in our fleshly bodies and to defeat the enemy.

The battle that we encounter from day to day is spiritual, not physical by a human point of view. By God's divine purpose for living in Him, the battle has been won. The victory starts on earth by accepting Jesus Christ as one's personal Savior. When we are born again, the soul patiently waits for eternity, to live with Jesus Christ, our Lord.

It was the end of June; I was glad the month was over. It had been a month of deep sorrow and pain, but my hope for today and tomorrow increased, as did my faith in my God for strength to live my life. I knew I had a purpose in life, and my legacy was to fulfill it while I had the time to do so. On the horizon, I saw the breath of new hope, the month of July. It would deliver a refreshing new energy to let me know I was alive and still trusted in God, my Creator.

Even though, I had received several negative responses from my applications for various positions, I still trusted God for a different outcome. When it was over, He received all the glory—hallelujah and amen!

Many people may recognize the month of July as freedom month, and what better way to be free than the only way I know—through

Jesus Christ, my Savior. His death on the cross did just that—He set us free! Sometimes our jobs or positions will hold us captive, and we are not free within. I know this because when I allowed my job to become first in my life instead of God, I was not free. For example, a weekend of mandatory overtime, over which I had no control, meant I was not free! I had to work instead going to church. During the weekdays when I did the overtime, I was too tired to attend midweek church. I was not free; I was still in bondage.

Physically and spiritually, the chain of slavery has become modernized for each generation. It has created a perplexed mind that seeks to take total control of one's body, mind, and soul, with a false impression of freedom each day. But one is not free because one's job is in control of one's life.

CHAPTER 11

◆

God Will Take Care of You

M y next in-an-instant moment was frightening and dangerous for me. It was in early spring 1978. I drove my father's pickup to work in my hometown of Louisville, Georgia. While at work, I looked out the front window of the building and saw threatening rain clouds forming in the direction of my parents' home. After I finished my shift at work around six o'clock that evening, I headed home.

As I drove, I noticed the volume of rain that had fallen in a short time. Immediately, my safety-alert antenna went into action. I knew that driving my usual route home was out of the question. My parents lived on a dirt road; the road that led to their house had red-clay soil for a substantial portion of it. After a hard rain, like the one that just had fallen, driving on red clay was dangerous, and the best of drivers could easily slide into the ditch. So, I took the next safest way home—at least, I thought it was.

The daylight was quickly fading away as I tried to get to my parents' home before dark. Sometimes the best plan is not the one to use at a moment's notice. As I approached the shortcut I planned to take, I had to drive on a short incline made of red clay, and it was as smooth as glass. As I approached the incline, I accelerated the pickup with just enough speed to conquer the hill and not slide into the ditch, but no sooner had I cleared the incline than a large puddle of water appeared out of nowhere in the middle of the road.

I had no time to decide what to do. I hit the large puddle of water with such force that water splashed all over the windshield of my daddy's pickup—and I did not have the windshield wipers on at the time of impact. Consequently, I was blinded by the wall of water that hit the windshield, and the pickup went into the ditch. This was the very thing I'd tried to avoid, but to no avail did it worked out the way I had planned it.

◆ ◆ ◆

This was just like life—we plan to do the right things, but then, life takes us by surprise; it happens in an instant. We want it to be different, but life doesn't always take the path we desire. When things like this happen in life, we have two choices that we can build on—one is for the good, by staying positive; and the other is for the bad, by seeing it as a negative. The choice is up to each of us to decide for ourselves. Which one will it be?

◆ ◆ ◆

I learned a valuable lesson on my evening drive home, and that was to have my wipers on delay, even when it does not appear to be raining enough to do so. I decided that I should not take away anything negative from this experience. Things in life happen for a reason. Sometimes that reason may reveal itself; other times, it may not. My lesson to embrace was to learn and grow to be better as a human being. It might build character, and I could sharpen myself into my purpose in life.

After pausing for a moment to get my thoughts together, I tried rocking the pickup, back and forth (by shifting to drive and then reverse, repeatedly), to try to spin my way out of my dilemma. But it did not work for me. My next move was to walk the rest of the way to my parents' house. It was now dark, and I had to walk about two miles or more to get there. Praise God, I made it safely and told my parents and family what had happened. Shortly afterward, one of my brothers drove the tractor to the pickup and pulled it out of the ditch—and I drove very carefully to my parents' home. On that day, I learned a great lesson: never drive a vehicle into a large puddle of water at a high rate of speed. It is too dangerous; anything can happen in an instant.

In July 2016, I had another in-an-instant moment. As I was getting ready for church on the first Wednesday, I also was heating something to eat and answering my e-mail on my cell phone. I placed a skillet on the stove top, and sprayed it with canola oil, and then walked into the bedroom, still answering e-mail. I got distracted and forgot about the fire under the skillet on the stove. As I walked from my bedroom, still distracted, a thought entered my mind, and I saw the reality of life flash before my eyes!

I looked toward the stove and saw the skillet on the stove with the fire burning beneath it. Instantly, something amazing and miraculous happened. The skillet that I had sprayed with oil was not smoking, burning, or on fire, yet when an oiled pan is over a fire for a short while, smoke will soon follow. To add to this miracle, the oil in the pan had consumed with little or no evidence any oil had been in the skillet at all.

I reached for a damp dishcloth to remove the skillet from the stove top. The handle of the skillet was so hot that it burned my finger. I placed the skillet in the sink and ran cold water onto it. I had to give praise to God for preventing a fire from taking place in the kitchen.

◆ ◆ ◆

It is so amazing how quickly life can change in an instant. An essay comes to mind that I wrote in January 2016, titled "I Dare to Rest":

> I dare to rest when I see my brothers and sisters from afar, journeying through the challenges of life in pain, along with their emotions, like the appearance

of a beaten and battled disabled ship (not able to sail but only to sink).

I refuse to rest, my brothers and sisters. Many of you are challenged by a broken, fatherless home, left to defend yourselves against the enemy of poverty on your own. Your emotions are rising high, like an eagle taking flight into the sky, searching for a peaceful place to rest. As you take flight, you want to live and not die.

The depth of your pain leaves you with an oasis of loneliness. It flows like a stream of water into the darkest night as you cry and cry, until the morning replenishes you with a new hope and vision for a new day.

I refuse to rest, my brothers and sisters. My pen I will put to paper to derail hate and the pain of life, by taking heed of solid wisdom and sound advice in Jesus Christ. It will be a witness to my fellow humans for eternal life.

The season of pain reaps a harvest of blessings in each day you live, in faith to praise and worship Him continuously. Do not try to go it alone in life to live free from sin, for the Savior, Jesus Christ, knows the avenue you need to journey on to endure until the very end.

I dare to rest, my brothers and sisters, for in Jesus Christ, each day, you will win!

The beauty of it all is in knowing who you are and whose you are. This will encourage you to leave a legacy for another generation to become influenced and inspired and to live by day after day. In-an-instant moments can be close—even as close as your front door. I experienced it one day in June 2016.

◆ ◆ ◆

My family and I had gone to see the movie *Samson*. Just as we were sitting down, an elderly man walked into the theater. He said to me, "My wife fell this morning."

"I'm sorry to hear that," I said. "Is she OK?"

He said, "She is here at the theater." The man then thanked me—sometimes we just need someone to listen—and then proceeded to go to and sit down with his wife. They just happened to be sitting in the row directly in front of us.

The movie was amazing on all levels. The actors, sound effects, songs, decor, makeup, and real animals made everything come to life. When the movie ended, the audience immediately started to leave the theater. I stood and proceeded to walk down the steps. As I was walking, I felt the guidance of the Holy Spirit, telling me to assist that elderly couple down the steps. I extended my hand to help the elderly woman, and I noticed that her husband was elated by my assistance for his wife.

Once at the bottom of the steps, the man smiled and thanked me for helping.

◆ ◆ ◆

I had never seen that couple until that day at the movies, and I've not seen them since then. Sometimes in life, our actions leave a profound impact on someone else's life, and that individual, perhaps unknowingly, did the same in return. Consider that as one sows, so shall one reap. An in-an-instant moment of showing the love of Jesus Christ to strangers will leave an impact and a life legacy to teach the next generation how to live with each other in harmony and love.

◆ ◆ ◆

In July 2016, I was filling out, on average, three or more job applications per week and still had not found a full-time position. The most difficult part of the process was the waiting.

One day, I received an e-mail about a position for which I had applied, and I thought it must be requesting an interview. When I read the e-mail, however, I realized it was another disappointing response: "Thank you for your interest in this position, but we chose another candidate for the position."

It was discouraging to go through that, day after day, but my faith in God kept me anchored and grounded until the day I received a positive response. Seeking a job was extremely demanding work. It was physically challenging (driving, walking, and seeking), emotionally challenging (waiting on the response, preparing myself for the interview), and mentally challenging (focusing my mind to say and do the right thing). I had to do daily searches, regardless of the outcome.

I learned that in addition to filling out applications online, I also was required to create a profile of myself, just to get the communication process started. Sometimes, I had to take an assessment test, and if I did not pass the test, I was disqualified from the application process. Then I'd be placed on a waiting list for about six months or longer, with some companies.

In an instant, my life was turned upside down. It was devastating to live until a positive breakthrough was delivered to reassure myself. I wondered, *With all the paperless applications, what socialization skills are we teaching the next generation of leaders?* The future generations would be challenged when holding conversations with other human beings. *Making eye contact and speaking face-to-face builds self-esteem and confidence in oneself,* I thought. *That's an old-school experience.* The following questions entered my mind: Are we heading in the right direction for the next generation to follow and be competitive? Are we teaching with the best tools so that our children will learn at the appropriate levels?

CHAPTER 12

◆

The Pain from an Odious Act

M any in-an-instant moments can come at lightning speed. This happened to me on an early-spring Saturday morning.

I had gone to church for a meeting. After the meeting, I planned to purchase gas on my way home. I had a gift card for a particular gas station, so I took a longer route home so I could stop at that station. The amount of money on my gift card was seven dollars, but I wanted to purchase twelve dollars in gas.

After arriving at the gas station, I noticed a sign: PAY INSIDE BEFORE PUMPING. It was chilly that spring morning, so my walk was brisk to the front entrance of the store. Once inside, I looked at the cashier, and it happened—I felt a quickening in my spirit. Why? I didn't know. Something like that didn't happen often, but when it did happen, I took notice of it.

I waited for my turn to pay for the gas. When the cashier signaled for me to come forward, I showed her the gift card, and said, "This gift card has seven dollars remaining on it, but I want to purchase twelve dollars total." I handed her a twenty-dollar bill and the gift card, and she gave me my change. As I was walking away, counting my change, I noticed that the cashier had not given me the correct change. Instead of fifteen dollars in change, she'd given me only eight dollars.

I quickly went back to the cashier to let her know about the error.

That was when the cashier became disrespectful and rude. I tried to explain that she'd given me incorrect change, but this cashier was the most discourteous person I had ever encountered at a retail store level. She reached in the cash drawer, handed me my twenty-dollar bill, and said, "If you do not leave, I will call the police!"

To this day, I still wonder what I did wrong. Being a peaceful person, I accepted my money and gift card and started to leave the store, but as I was leaving, I noticed the incident had been recorded on an overhead camera.

I decided to turn my situation over to another employee. "Could I speak to the manager on duty?" I asked her.

The employee said, "She's not in at this time."

I didn't know whether she was telling the truth—I had worked as a manager for two major businesses, and a manager was always on duty—so I asked for the store manager's name and the number of the store, which she gave me. I left the store without purchasing any gas—but I still needed gas. I went across the street, where there was another gas station. I soon realized that the credit card I used for various purchases was connected to the same business that owned the gas station with the disrespectful employee.

I would not soon forget the unpleasant experience with one of their employees, which left a bitter taste in my mouth. Even to this day, I often think about the episode at the gas station. In an instant, it changed my life forever.

On the following Sunday, I tried to contact the manager of the store but to no avail. The following week, I also called the business' corporate office to voice my concern, but nothing came from it. Customer Service did not appear to be a priority to the company.

◆ ◆ ◆

It is sad when a business allows their employee to mistreat a paying customer. To this day, I have not done business with that company since then. I was told that the recording of the incident on that morning *just disappeared* without a trace; I find that hard to believe. This led me to close my account with that business.

The integrity of a business is found in the services they provide their customers. In the business world of the twenty-first century, respectful customer service seems to have sailed away with the wind. I know this because I always gave top customer service, saying things like the following:

- Thank you, madam [sir].
- Welcome.
- Hello.
- Come back to see us.
- Have a great day.
- How can I help you, sir [or madam]?
- Here, let me get you a fresher one.
- I am sorry, madam, this item is about out of date. Let me get you another one.

In contrast, stores sell products that are out of date. Since the price is not on most items, some stores will scan a different item than what you purchased. It could be higher or lower in price. (Please check your grocery receipt to be sure you paid the right price.)

This happened to a family member just few days after Christmas 2021. My wife had gone to buy items for her electronics. After she returned home, I noticed the items cost almost sixty dollars. She checked the price on one of the items on the store's website, and the cost was twenty dollars. When we checked the UPC code, we found it did not match the UPC code on the receipt or on the product packaging.

She then called the store to tell them what we discovered, and she later returned the items. She then was able to repurchase them at the online prices.

My question is this: how often have consumers seen items at one price but pay a different price at the cash register? Countless retail stores may see this as OK, but it is wrong. This is stealing from the customers, right before their eyes.

Whenever a business takes shortcuts, part of that business dies a slow death. The services that many businesses formerly offered their customers at no charge now have a price tag attached. From a business perspective, it does not seem important anymore to give something back to the customer, regardless of the customer's length of patronage—days, weeks, or years on end. Instead, the business takes from the customer to reach their goal and profit margins, even though it is wrong. This is another way to steal and get away with it. I know this because I worked in retail for twenty or more years. I could write a book on retail businesses, prices, and assorted items that are on sale or supposed to be on sale.

CHAPTER 13

◆

Nobody Wins with Hate

In the second week of July 2016, there was pain, hate, and suffering to our nation and the world. On July 7, we witnessed the killings of four policemen and one other officer by one man determined to cause pain in a deadly way. Also, two civilians were killed prior to the killings of the five police officers. To some, the killings of the police officers were justified because the police officers killed the two civilians.

The truth of the matter is that nobody wins in a situation that represents hate; in some way, we are all affected by hate crimes. We all suffer from it, no matter how we may try to justify or deny it.

As a nation, we felt this emotional pain on a greater level. It reached the hearts of our fellow humans, whether male or female, young or old.

We need to see where we are as human beings and as a nation. In crises, we seem to come together for a moment or a season. But in reality, are we willing to change our way of living? We cannot expect things to be different if we do the same things over and over but expect a better result. It will never happen; we need to change from within.

I have learned from reading about history that we must look deep within ourselves and ask God to help us make that change from within. It must be from the inside out, not outside in. Only with God's help can we make true change.

I often reflect on my childhood days in Louisville, Georgia, a small farm town. In the downtown area is an old landmark building. It is beautiful to some, but to those who know the true meaning of its previous purpose, it is a symbol of pain, hate and an emotional reminder of what it once was. As a little boy growing up, I did not know the meaning that was nestled on the ceiling of that building, but later, I learned of its purpose, and today, it's a reminder, a painful witness in history.

Its purpose in Louisville was a place where human beings were sold as slaves to work on the many plantations around Jefferson County and Burke County, Georgia, and other places. As painful as it is for me to acknowledge, it will always be part of my life history, but not my life. I am a living, breathing child of the highest God. Louisville will always be my hometown; I cannot change that. But the path I chose is of love and kindness, not hate, sorrow, and pain.

I thank God for my parents. They are no longer here on this earth, but their legacy lives in me. Because of their teachings and love for my siblings and me, we were raised in a Christian home. My parents taught us to be people of truth and integrity and to love others as God had purposed our lives to do. In order for me to do this, I had to know the Savior, Jesus Christ, for myself. I refused to allow a landmark building to dictate to me the way I should live my life. I decided not to base my life on what was. Instead, I would do what I could in life to make a change for the better for all fellow human beings, through the guidance of the Holy Spirit, every day that I live, for as long as I can.

Even though I know the purpose of that building and what it represents, I cannot allow myself to embrace such a hateful and cruel reality or allow it to become a negative memory of my hometown history. Hate does not have a place in my heart of as a part of my characteristics as a person. There is no room for such a backpack in my life. This goes for the luggage we carry through life as well.

This is part of my personal life, and I can choose what is right. I live to be a productive person in society When I allow negativity into my life, I am spinning my mind, body, and soul, hoping for something better to bring about a positive change in my life. But better is delayed, because I have refused to allow a change opportunity of this magnitude to take place in my life.

There is no positive progress seen by my action if my action displays nothing more than hate. To change for the better, I must change as a person. Only God can truly bring about a change because it begins in the mind and moves to the heart, equipping my soul for the destination of eternal life. It is as simple as A, B, C—*accepting* the Lord and Savior, Jesus Christ, *believing* that Jesus Christ came to save humankind, and *confessing* and asking for forgiveness of my sins. Then I can have the reassurance that a change will follow into another generation, no matter what the color, age, and gender people may be.

History will be told in various writings for years to come, a witness for all to see, read, and learn. There will be teachable moments for future generation to use and grow differently than the way the previous generation was taught, but it starts with self.

I wrote the following based on the tragedy of 9/11:

Wounded and Inspired
A tribute to 9/11/2001

It was this day in history when our hearts, faith, hope, love, and dreams that rest deep within us were put to the test. The humbleness of various individuals retreated to the one haven, the church of our Lord and Savior, Jesus Christ. A place for the soul of humankind to receive real peace.

The spirit of humankind felt the pain of this odious act on that day. It was from the pilots and planes making their targets to kill lives and destroy the Twin Towers by creating a fiery explosion in the blue sky. The impact dismantled and melted reinforced steel with intense fire. The walls of solid concrete cascaded to rest on the dusty ground as deadly powder dust.

This extraordinary piece of history was erased, and volume of precious lives vanished (changed and perished) in minutes but were never to be forgotten. The pain transitioned into teardrop paths, erasing powdery dust that adhered to the faces of brave men and women who rushed to help. In contrast, many also rushed to escape the chaos, fear, pain, and death. As the world watched in disbelief, many courageous men and women laced their boots to defend and secure the sky, also in vehicles by land, by ships on rugged sea, and on ocean high to defend and protect America, the land of the free.

The power of this mighty force displayed a capital U, in a glorious representation called, Unity. During the chaos and pain, we raised the United States flag in love, defending and protecting American lives around the world. We are the Stars and Stripes built on the foundation of freedom for all, every day. Let it be known, humankind, that our hearts were shattered like crystal under pressure, like soft red-rose petals twirling slowly to the dusty ground. But in our faith, the spirit of humankind soared like an eagle taking flight, piercing the atmosphere with clarity, even in such a violent storm.

In Unity, our faith and love will always stand strong, like a mother waits for her baby to be born. It is the power of endurance. Embrace this freedom, my brothers and sisters; your faith still stands! It is about freedom, every woman and man. Put your trust in Jesus Christ, a faith to inspire the present and future generations to come. Then our rest will be in our eternal home (not made by mortal hands) with Jesus Christ. Let us visualize this perpetual peace, love, and freedom, not for a moment but throughout eternity. Then we can honestly say, "This is sealed by the Master's touch of creation" that we show love to our fellow humans. It is not in crisis alone but each day of our lives with His love and peace, until the end of time.

CHAPTER 14

◆

The Beauty of Love

I have another in-an-instant moment—my love story.

As little children grow, they are curious about many things. They one day come to the realization that love is a major part of life. It brings about new hope, dreams, laughter, and another generation to teach and love in life. Most people desire to be married and have a family to share their love. I also desired to have that kind of life to enjoy and to share my love with others. It was difficult, at times, when challenges became a reality. When I was growing up in Georgia, it seemed impossible at times, but God showed me differently.

On August 11, 1999, three pastors and I went to a church camp in West Middlesex, Pennsylvania. It was the first time for me, and the blessing was, I met my wife to be at the church meeting on Augusta 12, 1999.[1] This story is to let my brothers and sisters know that love came to me on a spiritual and physical level when I desired it in faith. It beautified and enhanced my life for another chapter to be shared in the world. It also showed others' love toward me as I continued my life journey.

Love Is Like a Rainbow

---

[1] You can read my true story in the book titled *The Sweethearts of Zion Hills*, a SOZH publication.

Love is like a rainbow; it comes in many colors. You too can be like a rainbow whenever and wherever you show love to others. Love is always liked, whenever it is done right. Take some time to show love, both day and night. The power of love will never, ever die, for Jesus Christ gave the ultimate sacrifice. When you share love with others, you will help to combat doubts and myths about hate and love. The greater of the two is love.

In an instant, my life was changed—a new chapter to write about love. I understood because the Holy Bible spoke of such action: "The greatest of these is love!"

Why do we all search for love? Many have died for it. Many have written songs, poems, and stories about love. Many have committed their lives (in marriage) to love, not knowing what awaits them in the future. The Holy Bible speaks, in a spiritual way, with such assurance that love is the major connection in life. This is so true because the Creator of life is God, and He is love!

This is for humankind, for the present and future generation. The one person who described and displayed love like this is Jesus Christ, our Lord. I praise you, my God, for sharing Your love to show humankind, day after day. This world can use the greatest dose of Your love to be a better world, for all and to all. There is power and blessings in the act of love toward others.

◆ ◆ ◆

On July 18, 2016, I woke early to pray and write words of encouragement. After the previous day's news about the shooting of yet more police officers by another veteran; this was expressed because of hate. The world needed to be inspired and encouraged to stop the violence and hate toward one another. The key part to this equation was the mindset of individuals who showed that level of hate toward another human being. At 3:15 a.m., it was a very peaceful time to write. I enjoyed doing so early in my day. I loved to write because the Lord spoke to me on a spiritual level, and I would listen with my spiritual ears tuned into heaven. I often didn't want to get out of bed, but I had learned to be obedient to God or risk losing what He had given me to write.

So, I committed myself to God; in doing so, He gave me something to write. I would do my part and write it. There were times when it might be a design to create; another time, a poem or reading to write. I was so grateful I had a willingness in my heart to do so for life. It was a blessing to help another human being, someone I might never meet or see in my lifetime.

These words could become a part of history and a testimony to the present and future generations. It could very well be the connection for the next generation when they need an outlet to plug into for their spiritual power shortage. This was one of my reasons for writing into the late-night and early-morning hours: to reach another generation.

CHAPTER 15

◆

An Act of Summer Kindness

A nother in-an-instant moment will always be a great part of my life. It is based on the Golden Rule: Do unto others as you would have them do unto you.

It was a sizzling summer afternoon in the red-clay hills of Georgia. I had gone back to my home church for Sunday services. Immediately after church, I visited with my parents and then started my drive back to Augusta.

I usually traveled by way of my hometown, Louisville, Georgia, a peaceful place to farm, retire, and enjoy country living at its best. After traveling on the dry dirt roads, my vehicle became very dusty, so I interrupted my journey to drive through a carwash; then I continued my drive back to Augusta.

On this particle Sunday, I decided to take a scenic route along a county road. The road's surface began as asphalt but then changed to gravel, which still was not as dusty as most dirt roads. After driving for few miles, however, the gravel road changed to dirt. Now I had two choices: (1) to continue on, or (2) to turn around and go in another direction. Because I'd just washed my car, I chose to turn around, go back to the highway, and continue on my way.

I later asked myself, *Why did I choose to travel that way back to Augusta?* Only God knew the answer because what I was about to encounter had to be divine intervention.

I turned onto a side road and had driven for less than a mile when I came upon a red convertible sedan parked on the shoulder of the road. I slowed down as I drove passed and saw a man and woman seated inside. Once I had driven by their car, a thought came to mind to offer my help, so I turned my car around and drove back to assist them. I parked my car behind the couple's vehicle. They were seated in their car, as if they were waiting for someone to show up to assist them. I asked, "Do you need any help?"

"We have a flat tire," the man said.

After examining the situation, I said, "I'll change the tire for you." We chatted as I worked on the tire, and I asked him, "Do you live around here?"

"Not far from here," he said.

"I used to work at the Piggly Wiggly [a grocery store] in Louisville, Georgia," I said. "That was few years ago, but now I live in Augusta."

As I was changing the tire, it occurred to me that this couple was quite elderly, possibly in their nineties, yet this man was still driving at his age. Also, it was a sizzling summer Sunday evening after six o'clock on a road appeared to be less traveled than normal—not one vehicle drove past us on the highway as I changed the tire.

After I had finished, the couple thanked me and were on their way. It took me a few minutes to clean my hands, and then I, too, was on my way, heading in the same direction that the couple was traveling.

As I drove, however, I did not see the couple's car, even though there didn't appear to be any side roads on which they could have turned off.

Often in my life, I have reflected on that hot summer evening and the scripture in Hebrews 13:2 (KJV): "Be not forgetful to entertain strangers: for thereby some have entertained angels unawares."

I am grateful that I assisted that couple in a Christian way. Because of my parents' teaching, I learned how to treat others with compassion. On that Sunday, an opportunity manifested itself, and I was able to assist in the situation at hand.

It is a blessing to know your true purpose in life and to walk in it day by day, blessing others along life's way.

CHAPTER 16

◆

Never Ever Give Up

On July 21, 2016, I was still searching for a job. That Thursday morning—at 4:18, to be precise—I asked myself, *What is my purpose in life?*

We all have a purpose in life that we must fulfill, by the grace of God. You can find your purpose by staying on bended knees before God in daily prayer. Another sure way to find your purpose is to find something you love to do and give it your best, as you give it away. Here are some important examples: If your best is love, give it away. If your best is words of encouragement, give it away. If your best is praying and blessing the less fortunate, give it away. These are minimum examples to help you rise to your maximum potential.

It is more blessed to give than receive. (Acts 20:35 KJV)

The gift is inside you, waiting to be birthed on any given day, as a blessing to people around the world. It is a phenomenal blessing when you can recognize your gift and purpose for living. Your gift is always bigger than what you can see with your natural eyes because God has previsioned it through His spiritual eyes. God will always equip you with the things you need to serve in your purpose. He has predestined it as part of your life.

This is my own example: I experienced three things before my move to Columbus, Ohio. First, I lived in Augusta, Georgia, for nearly twenty years. For twelve of those twenty years, I worked in the frozen foods department of a grocery store. There were times when I asked myself, *Why am I in this cold department?* Little did I know at that time that God was preparing me for my move to Columbus—it gets very cold in Columbus, Ohio—by improving my ability to endure the cold.

Second, in March 1997, I enrolled in the Augusta Technical Institute, but was put on a waiting list. One night, after a difficult day at work, I had another in-an-instant moment. I walked to the mailbox to get the mail, and as I was flipping through it, I noticed an envelope from the Augusta Technical Institute; in my spirit, I knew what it was about. The letter started with, "Congratulations. You have been accepted to start your classes in Printing Graphic Technology." That was one of the happiest moments in my life. During my time in school, I was interviewed or filmed by different photographers and television crews—channel 6, channel 12, inside the classroom and outside the technology building at the Institute, and at the grocery store where I worked.

Third, after I moved to Columbus, Ohio, I was filmed by the company where I worked, and my photograph was published in the Dayton, Ohio, newspaper.

All this information is to let you know that God prepares His servants for their assignments in life. All of the above accomplishments led me to this plateau of writing this book.

When I moved to Columbus, Ohio, in 1999, I became a member at the Wilson and Fair Street First Church of God. Each week, we recorded the service on various platforms to be seen around the globe. I did not know at the time, but all the previous filming and photographs were preparing me for something I did not see but God knew all along—the video recording of the church services.

When you find your purpose, serve in it with passion. Then, your service will be appreciated and received wholeheartedly by your fellow human beings, to the glory of God. I am happy that my sleepless nights and commitment to serving others all my days will be welcomed and received by others. Whether I am here on this earth or have journeyed into eternity with my Lord and Savior, Jesus Christ, my purpose will have been served, and God will get all the glory.

CHAPTER 17

◆

Praise God, I Am Free

On Friday, July 22, 2016, I had a desire to share another of my writings.

When we don't recognize that we are in bondage, it becomes a great challenge for us to visualize ourselves being free. The Holy Bible speaks of this:

> And it shall come to pass in the last days, saith God, I will pour out of my Spirit upon all flesh: and your sons and your daughters shall prophesy, and your young men shall see visions, and your old men shall dream dreams. (Acts 2:17 KJV)

The following words, which I wrote on January 16, 2016, came to me after a dream:

One Mountaintop Dream

I looked over the edge of this earthly life into the valley below, known as the City of Peace. There, the color of one's skin was not a factor. It did not focus on the material things one had in the past. The various job positions that people held in their lifetimes were not allowed in this city. This city represented eternal unity, praise, and love. It displayed value in a glorious and spiritual way, not for a season or a moment but throughout eternity.

In this mountaintop dream, the physical body met the presence of eternity. Therefore, we were disrobed from earthly vessels and transitioned into the eternal spirit destination, to live in the glorious presence of God Almighty.

Take flight, my precious child, and rise into your everlasting role, to live forever, praising, worshipping, and glorifying forever the only one true and living God.

On this mountaintop dream, I saw that half had not been told of the beauty in eternity for humankind's eternal soul. In order for humankind to be complete, each one needs to meet at Christ Jesus's feet. This is a real peace with the one God, Lord, and King at last.

In Him, I am free from this old world, free from all pain, suffering, tear-filled eyes, headaches, heartaches, guilt, and the disappointment of life. I am finally free, as free as can be, for my soul has reached its resting place in the beautiful land of eternity. Hallelujah! Hallelujah! Praise God, I am free!

What is real freedom? The making of real freedom is change from within. You cannot have freedom if you do not have peace within yourself. Do not allow the troubles and situations in your life to become the steppingstones to destruction. Instead, allow the trouble and situations you encounter to become the building blocks foundation in which freedom can be displayed. Then, freedom becomes the solid foundation from which to teach others how to live life in a positive way.

The walls of your troubles and situations that you have

encountered will crumble at the forces of freedom because your victory is won in Jesus Christ.

There are times when we desire to be free but do not know how to get there from where we are standing. It will take great faith in Jesus Christ, from day to day, to get to this level of real freedom.

CHAPTER 18

◆

Encouragement on Life's Journey

I had another in-an-instant moment over thirty years ago. It was in mid-spring of 1988. I had started a new job that February with another grocery store chain. I worked the third shift, which ended at seven o'clock in the morning. I then would drive ten miles to my home each day, but I would get very sleepy about halfway home. Each day, however, by God's grace, I made it safely home.

One Tuesday night, I went to work and then got off on Wednesday morning, as usual. But unlike the previous mornings, instead of going home and going to sleep, I stayed busy throughout the morning. When time came to go to church at six o'clock that evening, my in-an-instant moment revealed itself out of the darkness of night.

My sister and I left for church around 6:20 p.m., the usual time. As I was driving on Milledgeville Road in Augusta, Georgia, the traffic was comparatively light. I assumed that was because most of the people had gone home for the evening.

When we reached the second traffic light at Gordon Highway and Milledgeville Road, an unusual thing happened. Although my eyes were open, and I was still able to function and drive, my mind took a rest. When I thought the traffic light had turned green, I pressed on the gas pedal, and we quickly were in the intersection. My sister yelled, "Stop!"

Instantly, I hit the brakes. We'd come within inches of the first lane of traffic heading southeast to my east direction. My actions frightened the drivers of those vehicles, as well as my sister and me. The drivers of the other vehicles did not proceed when the light changed for them to go. The incident had been too intense for them—and me—as I'd stopped just before colliding into the other vehicles.

As I pulled over and exited my car, instantly, the passenger spoke her mind, "What is the matter with you? Are you asleep?"

I could hear her, but my focus was disoriented. I was sorry for what had happened, and I believed I apologized to her. Afterward, my sister and I continued to church.

The next day, I returned to work but still thought about the incident from the night before. I was at a point of quitting my job because working all night was difficult and dangerous. I needed a day job!

Sometimes, life can take us to places where we wish not to go. But in the right longitude, we can find the right attitude (in God's timing) to grow to the next level of latitude in life.

CHAPTER 19

◆

God's Prevision for Life's Provision

That Friday evening, I was seriously debating whether to quit my job. My all-night work was getting to be too much to manage, and I did not want to risk my own safety or the safety of others.

I reported to work as usual. The minute I saw my manager, he said that he wanted to speak to me about a personal matter. He asked, "Do you want to go to a first-shift position?"

I was very much interested, so I asked him, "Which department will I report to?"

"The Dairy Department," he said.

Several thoughts raced within my mind. It was a new store and, new department and was closer to where I lived—those were all pluses for me. Of course, my answer was yes.

Over the years, I have learned to depend increasingly on God for life's situations, both the ones I understand and the ones I do not understand. I have learned to totally trust God in my life. Over the next ten years, I worked in that position until it was time to move on. Just when I needed a major change or an answer to a prayer, God stepped into my chaotic arena and changed my situation for the better.

◆ ◆ ◆

My in-an-instant moments have shaped and molded me for this time in history, when I wrote this book. The benefits to readers are in my experiences and testimonies, which I hope will encourage and strengthen you for life. I also hope to prepare you for the many tests in life that will come your way. This is my act of service to all of humankind. I hope that the impact from it all would be a great witness, to encourage the faint of heart, as well as to fortify everyone to a higher standard in life and challenge everyone to be a better person to all of humankind.

Many people go through seasons of hurt, such as loss of a job, loved ones, home, or material things. Many people deal with broken relationships, such as between a father and son. There are mother and daughter, husband and wife, girlfriend and boyfriend, and best friends too. These are hurting seasons, in one way or another, but these relationships can be revived in Jesus Christ.

A lack of intimacy, a broken relationship with God, the death of a loved one—the hurt is so real! How do you survive this kind of hurt and still be productive in society and maintain a sane mind and focus? On your own, you would not be able to do it. But by the grace and mercy of a loving God, you can continue to walk, by faith, in Him.

In-an-instant moments, like some I have experienced, help us to endure, stay sane as individuals, and withstand our seasons. I personally dealt with many of these moments as I wrote this book. Was it easy? No, but I have learned to walk with God and gain greater strength as He brings me through another day to live for Him. You know, it is all about Him!

◆ ◆ ◆

On Monday, July 25, 2016, I was on my way to a temporary staffing service in Gahanna, Ohio, to sign up as a temporary worker, hoping to be hired in a full-time position. I received a phone call later that same day, and it was good news—the temporary work agency had a position for me. I accepted the position, and on July 26, I went to work for the first time in nearly two and a half months.

This was one of the most powerful in-an-instant moments in my life because just when it seemed that all hope had faded away and died, God, in His perfect timing, answered my prayer.

The work was more difficult than my previous job, which I had held for over fifteen years, but I was earning an honest living, and I believed that God would smile and bless me for that.

◆ ◆ ◆

If you find yourself at a later stage in life, and it feels like you are starting over again, do not give up or give in to the situation. Continue to stay in the fight until the very end. Your new profound breakthrough might have entered your arena to inspire, bless, and encourage you to your destiny in life for Jesus Christ. As a witness for Him, you, too, can become one in life.

CHAPTER 20

◆

There Is a Price for Faith

We will always have good news and sad news in life. I once heard odious news about a priest who was told to get on his knees and then was killed inside a church in a foreign country. I must ask the world: What are we doing? Have we gone astray in our thinking? Where did we go wrong?

We need to wake up humankind and change the ways in which we think and live our lives. If we don't, there will be a price to pay, and that price will be our souls. When the sky rolls back like a scroll, and Jesus Christ returns for His children, will you be one of them?

A number of blood-washed ones are waiting for that day! Look and see how time has changed, people have changed, and the love of many has waned cold!

Humankind has eternal souls that will live forever. You can choose today whether that will be in heaven or hell. My brothers and sisters, do it before it is eternally too late. I wrote an essay many years ago titled "Wake Up, America!" I recently added to it, as follows:

> Do you see, America? God speaks to us in many ways. Perhaps He is telling us that the end of time, the end of our days, is near! Wake up, America!

There are fires, wars, earthquakes, tornadoes, hate, viruses, disappointments, killings, floods, deaths, divorces, abandonment of families, and robberies— and the list goes on. These things are embedded deep within the emotional fabric of our beings. Our lives on this earth do not last forever.

The soul of humankind, however, does last forever because the soul was given to humankind by a loving, caring, and living God at the beginning of time. Humankind, take a good look around, and you will see that our land needs to be healed, along with the people of this world. How do we heal our land?

In the Holy Bible, the book above all books, you will find the following verse:

If my people which are called by my name shall humble themselves and pray and seek my face and turn from their wicked ways: then will I hear from Heaven, and will forgive their sin, and will heal their land. (2 Chronicles 7:14 KJV)

This verse is so beautiful. It is better than a pop quiz when the teacher lets you use your textbook to find the answers. Our heavenly Father has done that for us, and the "textbook" is the Holy Bible. We are at liberty to open it at any time in our lives. Let us be wise and make the right choices in life, starting at this very moment.

We need to make sincere amends to the God of creation so that we can receive profound, healing consolation. Wake up, America. We are walking on the edge of life, it only takes an instant, and you and I could be in eternity. We have abandoned our first love (God) by filling our hearts with selfishness, hate, envy, jealousy, and strife. Many have said that it's too difficult to love when someone expects something in return. The beauty of Jesus Christ's historical legacy is that He loves us *despite* our shortcomings, mistakes, and sins.

We must receive Him to become more sincere about life, about things we can, cannot see, know and learn on our own strength. We need to wake up, America, along with the rest of humankind, because our day is filled with seconds, minutes, and hours that make them profound and divine. Contrarily, we are like sand in an hourglass, with each grain playing a part in the erasing of time. In faith, we can see eternal life waiting, like seconds to minutes to hours in a day. Wake up, my brothers and sisters; without Jesus Christ, there is no other way.

Parents who neglect their duties are driving America down the tracks of destruction. We need divine guidance in our lives, like the Holy Ghost and the Holy Bible, a book filled with instructions.

Wake up, America. The time is now at hand. It behooves all of us to wake up while we still have a fighting chance.

CHAPTER 21

❖

Angels Watch Over Me

In summer 2009, my family (my mother-in-law) and I were on our way to New Jersey to attend a niece's graduation, from high school. We decided to leave as early as possible. We started our trip on June 24 around 4:30 a.m. The weather was warm and clear as we left our home. I drove for a few hours, and then we stopped for breakfast.

Once back on the highway, we continued on our way, but an in-an-instant moment was a few miles away. As we headed east on Interstate 70, I did something that I normally did not do when I traveled—I missed my turn. Of course, I had to turn around and make the correction onto the right road.

We had traveled only a mile or two down the road when an in-an-instant moment happened. As I saw a semi-trailer truck coming toward us traveling westward on the interstate, my attention zeroed in on a round flying object in the air. It seemed to be made of steel or metal, and it was heading in our direction. It must have fallen off the truck or possibly flew up into the air after it was run over. I could see it spinning at a high rate of speed.

I could not do anything to prevent this object from hitting the vehicle. The traffic volume was high in all directions, so I couldn't move out of its way; I could only brace myself for the impact. It was only by God's grace and mercy that the design of the windshield stopped anything major from happening to my family and me. The object veered off the glass into the unknown.

I've often wondered if that situation would have been prevented if I had not missed my turn, but even now, I am reminded of how faithful God is to His children, every day. I see the results of the impact by that metal object whenever I wash that vehicle. It is etched in my mind as well, as a testimony and witness for life.

I am so thankful to God for giving me the desire and will to pray before beginning any trip or vacation with my family on the dangerous highways. Those in-an-instant moments do not fit into my agenda, but God knows all things. He knew it even before I was conceived in my mother's womb. He knew what I would do with some of my in-an-instant moments. My hope, dreams, gifts, and purpose for living all are to be a witness for Jesus Christ, to show humankind that God is real. He can see you and me through all situations we may face in life. God brought me through those in-an-instant moments to increase my faith in Him.

On August 6, 2016, God blessed me with a job. This job allowed me to be humble at a point in my life when I thought I was already humble. But God's grace and mercy showed me that things in my daily walk with Him needed to be improved so that I could be a better Christian. I asked myself many questions, such as:

Do I really depend on God?

Do I depend more on my job or my position that I have achieved over time?

Will I continue to trust God if I lose my job?

Will I still need Him after I have achieved my hopes and dreams?

In our hearts, we can live a life that is pleasing to society, but let the truth be told: only God knows one's true intentions.

The following was another in-an-instant moment that I did not see coming during my day at work. A coworker asked me one day, "What's the meaning of your car's license plate?"

That profound question deserved a profound answer. It also gave me an opportunity to share the Word of God with one of my coworkers. We had worked together for almost two weeks, and that was the first time he asked me that question. In God's time, however, he did ask.

It so happened that my license plate displayed these letters: ORMYSTP. That stands for *order my steps.*

> The steps of a good man are ordered by the Lord: and
> he delighteth in his way. (Psalm 37:23 KJV)

After sharing the Bible verse with my coworker, I felt in my spirit that it will stay with him as a witness for Jesus Christ. I am incredibly grateful that God gave me seven letters to use as a witness to the people of this world. All praises go to God for giving me the desire to be a creative witness for Him to the present and future generations.

This also gave me a business opportunity. A line of graphic-design apparel with that phrase is still in the works. The phrase was published in a devotional book called *Personal Time with God*; the cover of that book was created and designed by Isaiah's Art Design in 2000.

CHAPTER 22

◆◆

In the Fight until Life's End

On August 7, 2016, I gave praise to God for allowing me to be where I am at this stage in my life. I did wonder if I *wanted* to be at that stage and age in my life. In my carnal thinking, the answer would have been a big no, but in my spiritual thinking, the answer would be yes. My experiences have taught me valuable lessons on how to perceive and receive from the situations I face in my life. This inspired me to write the following essay.

A Focused Christian's Life

Are you troubled on all sides but still have joy within? Do you try to live your life free from sin? Today, you can learn how to depend. For it is only in Jesus Christ and the Holy Ghost that your new life can begin. Are you in distress or perplexed but not in despair; persecuted for Jesus Christ's sake but not destroyed? Welcome, my brothers and sisters, to the life of being a Christian. Are you lied to, mistreated, and put to many tests? Being a Christian, you will not settle for less. The power of God is still in control; you are already blessed! A Christian's life on this earth consists of these things. My brothers and sisters, fix

your eyes on the prize in Jesus Christ, and your focus
on Him will become your highest aim.

On August 8, 2016, another coworker noticed the seven letters
on my license plate and asked what the letters stood for. Another
in-an-instant moment was presented to me. I witnessed to him by
reciting Psalm 37:23 from the Bible: "The steps of a good man are
ordered by the Lord." I also said, "When the Lord orders your steps,
you will have fewer headaches and troubles to deal with alone. As
you go through life, you will have Jesus Christ and the Holy Spirit
to strengthen and guide you safely to your eternal home."

The next day, this coworker and I were working together when
he responded to an incident in a foul manner. He then made a
statement about death and going to heaven, which caused me to say,
"Only way to get to heaven is to know and receive Jesus Christ as
your personal Savior."

Shortly afterward, our conversation ended, but I hoped that I'd
planted a seed that day. Maybe another brother or sister would water
it to another level, and growth would begin within that coworker.

While I was working on this temporary job, I received a phone
call from another company about setting up an interview with them.
Then, I received a card in the mail from an employer, informing me
about his company's rehire that would take place within two weeks.
I felt the presence of the Lord answering my prayers in many ways.

For the many things He has done and is doing in my life, I
continue to give Him praise. It is amazing how God's timing presents
itself in an impressive way. I'd had that personalized license plate
for over twenty years.

One day, one of my neighbors asked me about my license plate,
wanting to know what the letters meant. I also took the time to share
the words of Psalm 37:23 with him—the Lord orders the steps of
a good man. He had been my neighbor for two decades, but it was
God's timing that brought everything into perspective. I made it
clear as a witness for God.

Not long ago, I had another in-an-instant moment in which I

witnessed to another neighbor. That neighbor often walked his dog through the neighborhood. It was a cold Thursday afternoon, and I had just returned from a funeral at church. No sooner had I backed my car into the driveway than this neighbor walked toward me, looking at my license plate. He seemed to be trying to guess the meaning of the letters.

Then it happened—another witnessing moment to be shared to the glory of God. I explained to him that the seven letters (ORMYSTP) were based on the scripture found in Psalms 37:23 (the Lord orders the steps of a good man). This opened an opportunity to witness about my Lord and Savior, Jesus Christ. I saw another greater opportunity that God had sent my way. Praise God!

During the week of August 15, 2016, the Lord was still blessing me in a miraculous way. On the temporary assignment I was working, my manager had offered me overtime four times in three and a half weeks.

◆ ◆ ◆

Do not tell me that God is not real because I know differently! He is real in my life so that I can be a witness to you in your life. There is joy in knowing the Lord and Savior, Jesus Christ, for yourself. He will give you peace of mind, joy in your soul, comfort, and calmness when there are storms around you. He will fill your heart with His love that will bring tears to your eyes from heaven above. I praise him not just for a day or a season but for every day of my life!

◆ ◆ ◆

As I was working, I experienced a new mindset toward my work as I served others. I saw my coworkers—the young, middle-aged, and elderly alike—people who were willing to learn or teach on a greater level and in a place at which they would work, at most, for four years. The reality is that they made a sacrifice for those years to better themselves for a greater cause in society.

It humbled me in many ways. I was grateful to have a job to go to each day, even though it was a temporary position, and it was a difficult job to do! Many did not have the patience or the attitude to do such a job and serve others' needs. It was a hot, sweaty, and fast pace. My position was to provide university students and faculties with moving, setting up their dorms, and office services so that their places of residence would be as comfortable as possible, as it would be their home for four years or more. It was a humbling and rewarding experience that would be with me for the rest of my life.

CHAPTER 23

◆

One of Life's Teachable Moments

We have teachable moments countless times in life. The question is, what do we do with such moments? On Sunday, August 21, 2016, I was reflecting on an in-an-instant moment that took place early one morning while I was working as a stock manager at one of the major grocery chains in Augusta, Georgia.

I had gone to work early to open the store for business. My typical day started with checking in the vendors. This allowed them the time to restock their products on the shelves, from previous sales. It also allowed me the time to do the necessary office preparation before business for the day. When those tasks were completed, I opened the front doors.

As I stood in the office, looking across the parking lot in search of the first customer, a little boy walked into the store alone. He was around six or seven years old, and whenever a child walks into a store without an adult, that child needs to be closely observed. As I watched him, a coworker was watching me.

I saw this little boy do something that is a major negative act in all levels of society. He took a pack of cookies and put it in his pocket. He did not notice, however, that I had been watching him since he walked into the store.

I confronted him, asking, "What do you have in your pocket?"

Without denying that he had anything in his pocket, he showed me the pack of cookies.

I had a major decision to make because I was the only manager on duty at the time. I chose to make this a teaching moment. I told him, "It's wrong to steal."

"I'm hungry," he said,

"I will purchase the cookies for you," I said, which I did.

After I sent him on his way, a coworker told me, "I saw what you did."

I never saw that little boy again, but I hope what I did on that day changed the path on which he was about to journey, perhaps for life.

◆ ◆ ◆

An opportunity may knock at your door for you to be a blessing to another human being, to change that person's life forever. Don't allow that opportunity to pass you by without you being a help to that person. At a crucial time in that person's life, you can change the course of his or her direction and be a major influence in his or her life.

There are little boys and girls who do not have a father or mother figure at home. Even though they may deeply desire for parents to be a part of their lives, many children do not know their parents. Sometimes this results in their performing negative acts, like the little boy did.

In society, it does not happen the way I desire for it to be for the number of children around the globe. It took me countless moments to realize that all boys and girls are not blessed with a two-parent home. I encountered similar issues with many coworkers and former coworkers. There are many opportunities out there. All I must do is take a moment to zero in on them, whenever they present themselves before me.

◆ ◆ ◆

Yet another in-an-instant moment came my way. One day, I was returning home from work around 4:00 p.m. I decided to stop by Michael's, a craft store, to purchase some art supplies. Just as I was walking across the parking lot, a lady called out to me.

"Excuse me, sir!" she said boldly. "Could I have some money to get something to eat?"

I took a moment to think about what to do. I remembered a previous encounter and a request for money for food. I gave that individual some money, and I later saw him purchase alcohol instead of food.

I praised God for the guidance of the Holy Spirit because it gave me the wisdom to manage such a delicate matter, in love. I told the lady, "I will not give you money, but I will buy some food for you at the restaurant across the parking lot." She agreed. We walked to the restaurant, she placed an order, and I paid for it. She thanked me and ate her food.

I often think about the encounter with that lady. I hadn't seen her before that day and have not seen her since then, but my hope that I influenced her life. It might have been a turning point in her life to become someone greater than who she was on that day. That is the reason I love to praise my God!

On Sunday, August 28, 2016, I thought of one of my little nieces, she is dear to me. I am like a daddy figure to her. She lived with me for a while because her dad was not in her life, as a dad should be. I thought of an in-an-instant moment when she was younger, about three or four years old.

Late one evening, we walked to the playground in the neighborhood where we lived. Once we arrived, I assisted her as she played on the seesaw, swing, and monkey bars. I held her as she reached for the bars; she was happy just to touch the bars while I did all the work to support her as she went from bar to bar.

The in-an-instant moment came from an uncle's or father's perspective. These were precious moments I never wanted to forget. My niece greatly enjoyed playing on the slide. Little did I know what was about to happen. I helped my niece to walk up the ladder on the slide, which was about six feet high, and I carefully watched as she started to slide to the bottom.

About halfway to the bottom, however, she tumbled over and went down the slide headfirst. Praise God that I was standing in front of the slide to catch her as she came down. Only God knows what could have happened if I had not been there to catch her from the tumble.

As I thought about that moment with my niece, another writing came to mind:

Where Are You, Father?

It is through a child's eyes. I am lying here on my hospital bed, very much alive but feeling dead, instead. Dead with volumes of emotions within my mind. I do not feel your love, Father. As I look around, you are nowhere to be found. I am thinking to myself, *This is a blessed day because it only comes once in a lifetime.* Where are You, Father?

I have just been born, and you are not near. My heart is breaking because your presence is not here. If only I knew that being a part of your life would have caused me such great pain, in my Father's Heaven, I would have remained. Where are You, Father?

I am lying here in bed, knowing deep in my heart that I need to be fed. I want to hear that you love me and not hate me, instead. This causes me such painful feelings inside my tiny head. Where are You, Father?

Once I came into your life, you did not give me your name. Your love for me has already changed. Sometimes my heart feels the fear, day and night. My eyes are flooded with tears. Please remain in my life throughout my precious years, for I am young, and these memories I will always hold dear. Where are You, Father?

I want you to be a great part of my life; I want to embrace your love without the strife. You are welcome to share with me your wisdom and sound advice. In my mind, this is so new. I want you to know that no matter what happens to me, I will always love you in my heart, the way it should be. This coming from me will always hold true. Where are You, Father? I truly do need you!

In this society in which we live, many children may feel this deep void (absence of a parent) in their hearts. They cannot express in words that which will change the parents from taking actions such as divorce or separation that will impact their lives forever. We are the adults who can shape or break the child from being productive in society. It is easily seen in what we do and say in our pressurized situations in our lives. Being a father, I have failed many times to get it right, but I praise God for His grace and mercy, He forgives (whenever I ask for forgiveness) as I learn from day to day.

I will face many in-an-instant moments until life on this earth has ended. Then, my legacy will impact others with whom I have or have not had contact. The beauty of my final in-an-instant moment will be witnessed by many, as how I received, believed, and lived my life in that moment.

Humankind has a void within that needs to be filled spiritually. Only what is spiritual can be filled by the Spirit. Many have tried to fill the void with material things or another human being—it will not work! The beauty is in knowing when there is a void and what it takes to fill it. The depth of that void is greater than what the human eyes can see.

I am grateful to know that in my spirit, I accepted the filling (Jesus Christ and the Holy Ghost) for my void many years ago. This void within humankind will never die because it is spiritual for the rest of our lives on this earth, into eternity. There is no substitute to fill this void within; only Jesus Christ can do it in a perpetual way.

I wrote the following in 2007:

The Void Within

Since the day of creation, there has always been a void that rests deep within the soul of humankind, a void that one can experience from day to day. There is no earthly thing or the presence of another human being with power to fill this void. This void is spiritual.

The human eye cannot see, nor can ears hear, but in faith, you can feel the presence of the Savior, Jesus Christ, ever so near. How rich and blessed you will be whenever you receive the fullness for this void. Nothing else can or will compare because your faith now embraces Jesus Christ, the Savior, who really cares.

I will face volumes of in-an-instant moments until my life on this earth has ended. Then, my legacy will affect others. The glory, honor, and praise will return unto the Lord and Savior, Jesus Christ, from which it came. Amen.

CHAPTER 24

◆

We Stand in Faith

When one has faith the size of a mustard seed, the preparation for eternity rises to the forefront as one's key focus and concern in life. The power of faith is how one seeks and applies this hope in one's day-to-day living.

Whether or not you and I believe, we are all living by faith on each given day.

> Now faith is the substance of things hoped for, the evidence of things not seen. (Hebrews 11:1 KJV)

There is faith in getting paid from a previous week of work in the current week. There is faith in hoping it does not rain before I can cut the grass; faith in hoping I do not run out of gas before reaching the gas station. We hope for things we do not see. That is faith! We live our lives surrounded by hope. That is faith! There is no need to desire it any other way. It does not matter what others may do or say. This is profound hope. It is here to stay. It is a blessing to be able to endure a test of faith with in-an-instant moments in one's life.

My wife, daughters, and I had to live through the following at one point in our lives: My wife and I had been married for seven years when we received some unwelcome health news. The lump was found at an early stage, but it was positive for cancer. The treatment that followed lasted for eight weeks.

At that time, we had two beautiful little girls. It was a blessing to receive such precious gifts from God and to be able to share them with others, in love. As parents, the joy from it outweighs the time spent in teaching and training the children to prepare them for life in this world. Both, my wife's father and my father had died by the fifth year of our marriage. I often wished that those fathers could have been there so I could have asked them questions about raising a family. How did they do this or that? How did they manage a situation from a father's perspective pertaining to young girls? It was sad that they were no longer with us.

Nevertheless, they did leave a legacy for me to follow. It was to train and teach our daughters to be beautiful and productive women in society. I fixed my focus on being a tenacious father, in love, to our daughters. Along with wisdom, I have taught them the right path in life by God's help. I believe they will become productive women one day.

This connector of pain and sorrow has reached our marriage borders and forced its way ashore. When something is connected to our marriages, by God's help, we can continue on, in faith, taking one day at a time. In contrast, when something is *in* our marriages, it can cause much chaos and confusion. God's is not the author of confusion (1 Corinthians 14:33) KJV.

I wrote the following essay in 2006:

Lie Still

My brothers and sisters, when the storms of life rip you to the core and the burden of life's journey gets heavier than the tallest mountain lie still in the arms of the Savior, Jesus Christ, and feel His love to make you complete. There is no problem too big or small. He has survived and conquered them all. Today, fix your eyes on the prize, and live strong in His might. You can do it by His grace, day and night.

You will survive, now and the rest of your life. Lie still in the arms of the Savior. There is peace filled with eternal rest when you feel you cannot pass all life's tests. Just remember your heavenly Father truly knows what's best, and that is one eternal reason you should not settle for less. Lie still, God's precious creation. You are still a part of His mighty plan.

When life is filled with great chaos and you do not understand, lie still in the arms of the Savior on His solid foundation, embracing His eternal plan. He is not like all the others who are sinking sand. This is a spiritual requirement. Today, you have the choice to take that stand, do it now, while you can. In the precious arms of Jesus Christ, you can lie still, my child, and not be in fear. He is forever near you from the beginning and ending of your years. Lie still my child.

In early spring of 2008, my wife told me that she felt a lump in her chest. She made an appointment to have a doctor examine her. The doctor took a tissue sample from the area where the lump was present. The sample was sent to a lab, and in a day or two, we had the results.

The test result was positive, meaning that my wife had breast cancer. From a husband's point of view, I wondered, *Where do we go from here?* In faith, I prayed, trusted, and believed God for who He is. It wasn't easy, and it did require discipline. God knew it all along that our faith would be enriched for the better as a witness for Him.

For the next eight weeks, I made it a priority to be there for my wife as often as I could when she went through chemotherapy to conquer the deadly disease. Because this happened in the early years of our marriage, I believe it strengthened our relationship to a greater level. In my heart, I took our marriage vow to heart when I said, "I do, until death we do part."

My mind was racing like a fighter jet, traveling greater than the speed of sound. Our daughters (praise God) received the news of their mother's illness at a more mature level than I could have imagined for their ages. There were times when my wife did not have the strength to do different things after her chemotherapy. I would tell the girls, "Your mother needs to rest." And they would let her do so; they wanted Mom to get better.

Sometimes, our faith is assessed at the least-expected moment and at times in our lives when we desire it not to be. But God knows everything—the past, present, and future.

CHAPTER 25

◆

I've Never Traveled This Road Before

On March 21, 2008, during my wife's illness, I wrote the following words about how I was feeling, spiritually, physically, mentally, emotionally, socially, and financially.

W ho would have thought, on this earthly journey in life, I would have to go through difficult and challenging moments with my wife and family? My faith foundation was shaken to its core but not diminished. One day, it reached our doorstep at the most unusual time in life—our marriage was young; we had two young daughters. In contrast, the deaths of our fathers were still fresh, with high emotions to deal with at various times in our young marriage. And while standing in the depth of my faith and being assessed, a thought rooted within my mind that spoke to me: *You have never traveled this way before.*

Who would have thought my strength, focus, determination, and the richest and precious gift known to me (my faith) would be assessed like never before in my life? The purpose is to strengthen and shape me to grow my faith in God. There is nothing else to compare or matter in my life at any given time. *I have never traveled this road before.* Who would have thought the pain, prayers, writings, readings, and teardrops that ran down my face would be the healing process I needed at this time in my life to grow? This was a miracle waiting in the wind to give me strength to mount up wings like an eagle and soar to new height in my faith walk with Jesus Christ. I had to trust Him at a new level in life.

I rehearsed it over and over in my mind, to try to find an answer to the matter at hand, but to no avail was an answer discovered. The lament that gripped my mind, and the teardrops that I shed from the many thoughts about my wife and family overwhelmed me. It raced through my thought process and would not vacate my mind. Therefore, I had to pray to God for more strength about our situation that was forthcoming. From it all, I have learned to trust Him more, in all matters in life.

Even though I cannot see Him, a new hope of faith has been birthed on the inside of me to be a true witness to humankind. I will share my testimonies to bless others as they encounter the many tests in life. This is love to the fullest and highest degree in Jesus Christ for humankind. I refuse to allow doubts and fears to take root and grow. In a fetal position during my storm, without God, I am weak! I cannot survive or stand to endure the many tests in life. The faith that I hold for dear life has outstretched His arms and body to die on the cross, so I could live free from sin. Jesus Christ showed the greatest depth of love known to humankind so we could be free in Him. The question is, who wouldn't serve a Savior like that?

Many times, I have tried to comprehend this in a world in which sin does exist. The enemy is equipped to hurt and destroy the mortal body, but it cannot touch the soul. God is still in control of it all. *I have never been on this path before.* Who would have thought, in seven years of marriage, this storm would be found on the street on which we lived? And positioned itself to stay a good, long while, but God's plan said, "It is different!" I have been told the number seven means completion. And if that is the case, my family and I are starting over again on this journey that we have never been before. I have received many wonderful gifts, such as family, material things, and making of friends in many ways, but nothing compares to the Salvation of Jesus Christ. I am complete in Him.

A thought comes to mind that lets me know I am still in a

spiritual battle, daily, fighting for my life. *I have never traveled this road before.* It was not just my faith being assessed but my family's faith as well. We felt the pain, emotionally, financially, physically, mentally, spiritually, and socially, but through it all, our faith in God stayed strong. Because He works things out in His time.

From the start, it was me being able to leave work early to be with my wife at her treatment appointments. And my wife was able to receive some financial assistance through her job. Who would have thought a testing of my faith would be with the ones I love and hold dear to my heart, God, and family? We were never alone. God had our back, front, and everything in between. We praise and glorify Him for dear life!

Volumes of questions and pain rose within me. But my faith, I still place in You, oh God, to show me what I need to do. My hope and dreams for life come from You. This day, I must be strong and stand on your promises.

> Moses said unto the people, Fear ye not, stand still and see the Salvation of The Lord, which He will shew to you today: for the Egyptians whom ye have seen today, ye shall see them again no more, forever. (Exodus 14:13 KJV)

For that, I must wrap my faith around Jesus Christ, the rock-solid foundation. In Him, I take my stand in the glorious rays of light to press on in this fight, never to faint or yield along the way. Because one day, the testing of my faith will give way to victory that is only found in Jesus Christ, our Lord.

My faith has positioned itself in a geographical way for the entire world to see. The feeling is like a dawning of a new day. The spirit of the wind breathes fresh air upon my soul for a newness to live because, by faith, eternity would have entered the arena and taken a stand on my behalf. Then I can sing a hallelujah praise, "Free, free, praise God, I am free!" *I have never traveled this path to eternity before thee, my God!*

CHAPTER 26

◆

Reflection of First Love to True Love

The power of first love is a force to reflect upon to see how much one may have learned between first love and true love. First love is like when one learns how to ride a bike. Some mistakes will be made, but one can learn from them and move on. And through it all, one's confidence in the relationship will grow as well. True love is like graduation—one has accomplished a major goal in life to become a better person. It is to receive and share like the value found in true love.

The following in-an-instant moment is personal in many ways. It is inspired by a true story, but the names and places in the story have been changed.

On a summer morning in the small town of Permville, U.S.A, just across the way, Jonathan watched the many buses as they entered the schoolyard. He knew this school year would be different. Shortly afterward, the bus drivers stopped to allow the students from the other schools to exit the buses. Sierra stepped off the bus and took a quick survey of the new school and the pool of students in her presence. The challenges and diversity of new students with whom to interact and learn was the fresh start she needed. She felt the high-energy vibes coming from the many students who were so eager to learn at a higher level than at the previous school they once attended.

What once was an elementary school had changed into a middle and high school. Many surrounding schools merged to become part of one big school, with new students of various ages and colors coming together. Jonathan watched the many students as they stepped off the buses.

In the distance, he saw an attractive new girl. She was beautiful and wonderfully dressed, with smooth, radiant skin, and she appeared to be around Jonathan's age. *This school year is going to be great*, he thought. At that very moment, Jonathan knew that he wanted to meet her.

When the school bell rang, all the students went to their homerooms. This new girl had gotten Jonathan's attention without knowing she had done so. For now, she was lost among the sea of students as they walked to their different homerooms.

Little did Jonathan know that his day was about to get interesting because the new girl was in some of his classes. In English class, Jonathan learned her name—Sierra—and that she was left-handed. He also noticed that whenever Sierra smiled, she had the most amazing dimples. Jonathan had a cousin who had dimples, but his cousin's dimples did not compare to Sierra's. To Jonathan, she won—hands down!

Sierra and Jonathan also were in history class together.

Over the next three years of middle school, Jonathan and Sierra seemed to cross each other's paths time after time. Each year, Jonathan became more interested in Sierra. He saw her transition from a girl into a beautiful young lady who was more fascinating to him each year. The question was, what was he going to do about it?

After the three years of middle school ended, Jonathan knew that high school would be different. He tried to prepare himself for ninth grade and the new school year. Jonathan knew he had to dress in more attractive clothes to impress Sierra.

One day, he encountered some students who were not pleasant to be around. They bullied him and called him out on his tennis shoes. Just because he could not afford name-brand tennis shoes, they called his shoes *jeepers*; in other words, the shoes were cheap— according to some of his classmates' standards. They were surprised to see him wearing such a pair of shoes to school. Jonathan was embarrassed and hurt by their comments, but he journeyed on because his focus was not on them but on school and Sierra.

That year, Jonathan finally got the courage to talk to Sierra. It was as simple as speaking and being nice to her. One day, Sierra's friend Beth was playing a friendly game called "I Command You." The game seemed simple and harmless but in a secretive way. The *secretive way* was based on not getting caught by the teacher. Jonathan had heard about the game and saw other students playing it with their classmates. Beth and Jonathan rode the same bus to school. She, too, had been in various classes with Sierra and Jonathan.

One day, when the bell rang for the next period, Beth and Sierra went to their next class and sat next to Jonathan. As they waited for the final bell to ring, Beth went into an *I Command You* game mode. She told Sierra, "I command you to kiss Jonathan!"

As Sierra and Jonathan leaned forward to do the command, the bell rang. They were "saved by the bell"! Also, they were just shy of being embarrassed or caught by the teacher; they both ceased their actions. On that day, Beth discovered something about Sierra; she had feelings for Jonathan.

Now things started to get Jonathan's attention, but he did not know that Sierra had feelings for him in a sweet way.

As the years in high school inched along, Sierra and Jonathan became good friends in many ways. One day, Jonathan received a note from Sierra, specially delivered by one of Jonathan's friends, Alex. As Jonathan read the note, he fell in love with her words and her fancy handwriting. He smiled and thought, *Her writing isn't bad for a left-handed individual.* Jonathan had always been fascinated by beautiful handwriting. He was grateful to God and his mother for that. His mother had amazing handwriting skills; it was like her hand just floated over the paper as she wrote. God had blessed his mother with beautiful handwriting, and Jonathan had inherited the gift as well.

By the end of the school year, just days before summer break would begin, Jonathan did some serious thinking on where he wanted to be in the next two years. Once the ninth-grade school year was finished, he would have all summer to think about it while helping his parents on the farm.

Farm life was challenging in many ways. It had many difficulties. There was much work to do. Various crops had to be harvested from the fields and then prepared before taking them to market. The animals had to be fed.

Shortly into the new school year, Jonathan thought about what to do after the tenth-grade school year. After much consideration, he decided to skip the eleventh grade and go directly to the twelfth grade because he had enough credits to do so. However, there were reactions from some of his classmates. Some said Jonathan would not be able to complete his classes and graduate in the new school year. Jonathan's response was, "Watch me. You will see!"

After his tenth-grade school year, the summer went by quickly. The new school year started, and Jonathan knew he had to apply himself to do his best and maintain a focus to finish strong. And that he did. Although Jonathan wanted to fulfill some goals in life, he had some sad and mixed emotions after his graduation. It was the feeling of not being able see Sierra in high school anymore.

After graduation was in the history archive of yesteryears, Jonathan's focus was on getting his driver's license and his first job. He had tried once before school was completed but had failed to pass the written exam. Nevertheless, his next attempt was successful. In a brief period, Jonathan made great progress on his short-term goals, but he was still searching and hungry for so much more in life.

In the late summer after his graduation, Jonathan decided to apply for his first job at the local grocery store. Sure enough, he received his first paying job. Each day, he went to work around eight o'clock and worked for six or more hours. Overall, his job was easy, and he interacted with and served many customers. Still, the one girl he liked the most had faded into the unknown.

Little did he know that Sierra's mother had been to the store where he worked. He had packed her groceries numerous times, but he did not see Sierra. Then one day, when he was busy working, he turned around and saw a girl with pretty dimples walking into the store, that girl was Sierra. Jonathan expressed a bright smile as he spoke to Sierra and her mom as they did their grocery shopping. Sierra made Jonathan's day better—oh, so much better!

The fall was approaching quickly; the weather has started to change. But one thing remained the same: the special feelings Jonathan had for Sierra. The sincerity of his emotions left him wondering what he should do about it.

Jonathan and Sierra had different goals in life. Jonathan was planning to move to another city and go to college. He loved art and design.

One day while at work, Jonathan was cleaning and restocking the grocery bags for the day's business. He took a moment to carry some groceries for a customer. As he was walking toward his customer vehicle, he noticed a car parked close to the exit door. A thought crossed Jonathan mind as he returned to the store; in one quick glance at the car's license plate, he memorized the number. It was a good thing he did because as he went back into the store, the manager called out to him, "Did you see the man who just left the store?"

Jonathan made a quick U-turn and went outside to look for the car, but the man and the car were nowhere to be seen. Once back in the store, the manager explained what the man had done to the cashier—he had confused her and stolen money from her. This was known as *flimflam*, an act of deception.

Jonathan quickly remembered that he had memorized the car's license plate number, which he told the manager. The store manager quickly called the store manager in the next town. The police were able to locate the man in the next town, trying to do the same thing to another cashier, but he was stopped. It was due to Jonathan's quick thinking in getting the car's license plate number. The phrase "See something; say something" holds true today.

Jonathan worked at his job for many weeks, hoping to get ahead in life by being more productive. He was committed to the company he worked for. Each day, his manager had noticed how dependable Jonathan was, even at such a young age.

One day, his manager called him into his office and had a conversation with him about a promotion to a stock clerk, with full-time status, a pay increase, and benefits. Jonathan was grateful for the promotion and thanked his manager for considering him for the position. Nevertheless, Jonathan felt that he was much more than where he was in life.

Jonathan's work schedule was more challenging than his previous one, but he was determined to stay committed, as he had always been. After several weeks of working his new schedule, Jonathan concluded that he needed a car. Immediately, he increased his weekly savings so he could buy a car. After few months, Jonathan had enough money to get the car he wanted, and he paid cash for it.

After buying his car, Jonathan had the responsibility of maintain it. Some of the maintenance was changing the oil, washing and cleaning the car, getting tune-ups, and replacing the tires. The list never seemed to end. But Jonathan's accomplishments outweighed the simple upkeep of his car. He was incredibly pleased with his purchase.

He thought about Sierra and what her reaction would be to his purchase. Things went a different route when it came to his car.

Jonathan knew it was time for him to move to another level after he got a promotion on his job. He asked for a transfer to a larger city, and his request was granted. However, he had another plan in mind—like asking Sierra on a date to a county fair before moved to the big city.

One day, he got the nerve to ask Sierra on a date, and she accepted. The last day before leaving for his new job, Jonathan and Sierra went to the county fair. They had a wonderful time and even won some prizes. After taking Sierra home—it was nearly midnight—Jonathan went home and went to bed.

Jonathan made it home safely, only by the grace and mercy of God.

Early on Sunday morning, Jonathan planned to go to church; afterward, he would drive to the city, his new place to work. However—praise God—when he went to start his car on Sunday morning, it was as dead as a doornail. Jonathan realized that only God knew how he had made it safely home without anything happening to Sierra, him, or his car. He gave all the glory and honor to God because he was a man of faith.

Jonathan and one of his brothers tried with all their might to get the car started, but to no avail; it had a dead battery. Once he installed a new battery, he would be ready to travel. Early Monday morning, his brother drove to town to purchase a new battery. Jonathan still had to drive for an hour to be on time at his new job. Quickly, he retrieved all the things to take with him and put them in his car. And in an instant, he was gone.

After some serious driving, Jonathan arrived safely to his new place of work. The first workweek went smoothly, and he became familiar with the city and his new surroundings. His new coworkers were easy to work with and willing to help in a caring way. The transition he had made looked increasingly promising. This made Jonathan feel more positive about himself; he always felt something inside himself that encouraged him to rise to the challenges of life. Little did he know, a great challenge was just over the horizon.

One day, about three weeks after Jonathan had moved to the new city, he was leaving work when he noticed something strange about his car hood. Jonathan's heartbeat increased. He had an empty feeling in the pit of his stomach. He did not want to think about what he might find.

Slowly, he lifted the hood and saw that his new battery was gone. Jonathan felt sick; it was a bad feeling like none he had ever felt before. Nothing of value had even been stolen from him before. After finding out he had been robbed, Jonathan reached out to one of his brothers for assistance, and his brother took him to get a new battery for his car. Quickly, they installed the battery, and afterwards, they both were on their way home.

Jonathan knew some things had to change for his safety. He was no longer in a small town where everybody knew one another. He had to put up his guard in every aspect in this city. The people were not as friendly as in his hometown. Therefore, they could not be trusted in many cases. For starters, he had to lock his car doors at night. He could not leave valuable personal items lying around in the car, at work or at home.

As the weeks transitioned into months, things started to look more like home to Jonathan. His coworkers shared with him the dos and don'ts around the city and told him which places to visit and not to visit, especially at night in his sports car. Each day, he took his coworkers' advice to heart to stay safe.

The memory of Sierra started to fade like the setting sun, moving dimly into the unknown (but not forgotten) because Jonathan and Sierra had gone their separate ways after graduation. He wondered if their paths would cross again. Would they talk about their date from the county fair? Would they ever see each other again? There were so many questions and no answers. What would Jonathan do?

CHAPTER 27

◆

A Manager for Danger and Challenges

Jonathan continued to prove that he was worthy of a promotion because he was a responsible, productive, efficient, and ambitious employee. With qualities like that, he knew it would only take a few months for the reward to become a part of his credentials. Four months later, a promotion was knocking at his door.

Jonathan was offered a job as an assistant produce manager. Of course, he accepted the offer and the challenges that came with the promotion. After a few months in that position, another opportunity presented itself; he was offered another promotion to become an assistant stock manger. Once again, he accepted the offer.

In his new position, he supervised six of his coworkers in ordering, restocking the grocery shelves, and daily cleaning up of the store. This position had many challenges, such as restocking the shelves in a timely fashion. As he collaborated with coworkers who were older. Jonathan displayed leadership at a greater level than his coworkers. He had brief meetings with his team, offering instructions and directions on what needed to be done before the stock team could go home. One of his benefits was being able to leave early, before shift ended, but he enjoyed servicing customers face-to-face; it was a blessing and an honor.

One Sunday at home, when the store was closed, Jonathan received a phone call from the assistant store manager, who said that the store alarm had gone off and that he needed to check out the store and reset the alarm. Quickly, Jonathan went to the store and did a check of the store. The contrast between when the store was open for business and when it was closed was like night and day. When open for business, the store was loud, and customers and employees were as busy as bees on a honeycomb. When it was closed, the store was as quiet as a mouse. After Jonathan checked various things in the store, and everything looked to be OK, he reset the alarm and went home.

Shortly after the alarm incident, another dangerous matter was on the horizon, waiting for the right moment to present itself. One Wednesday morning, Jonathan had to open the store for the day's business. He arrived early to allow vendors to restock the shelves, and he prepped the store registers for sales. He hadn't been there for more than an hour when he happened to look out at the parking lot—and he could not believe what he saw. There was movement of legs going back and forth beside one of the delivery trucks, but the delivery driver was in the store. Jonathan had to investigate the matter at once to see what was going on; he knew something was not right, so he carefully and quietly exited the store. He walked across the parking lot and followed a young man. The man carried various items and placed them on the ground under the small bushes all around.

Jonathan confronted the man, and without saying a word, the man showed a weapon tucked in his pants. Jonathan didn't know if it was a knife or gun, but he slowly, stepped backward, while not taking his eyes off the robber. Once out of harm's way, he quickly went back inside the store. After a brief moment, he composed himself and continued to manage the store; he did not say a word about the matter. The thief had seen his face, and Jonathan feared for his safety. Thank God for wisdom.

After few months, Jonathan was offered yet another position, one that came with a greater challenge than before. He would have to leave the store at which he enjoyed working. The position was stock manager at a new store; he would be responsible for ordering, pricing and stocking. He accepted the new position. He soon found out it was demanding work and long hours, well into the night, to get the store opened, but his hard work paid off! Jonathan survived the challenge in his new position by meeting the deadline for the store to open. It took only three days.

The day of the store opening went off without a hitch. It was great for Jonathan and others to see their work was appreciated by the many customers. The first day had strong sales. After few days, things started to seem more normal, so Jonathan got a general idea of what the sales at the store would be; then he could order accordingly each week. The sales continued to be high, and the managers welcomed it. Jonathan and his team faced this challenge with determination and the right mindset.

After several weeks, things still were looking up—until early one Wednesday morning. Jonathan arrived at the store exceedingly early to get the store ready for the daily business. No sooner after the store opened, Jonathan was ordering product to restock the shelves with various grocery items. As he was working in one of the grocery aisles, a lady shopper walked down the aisle toward him, doing her shopping. Out of nowhere, a young boy came down the same aisle—and the lady shopper screamed. Instantly, Jonathan turned to see the young man grab the customer's purse and run.

Jonathan knew he had to do something quickly to stop the young man, so he reached out to grab the young man, but he missed him. Now, the chase was on.

It so happened that Jonathan had worn his tennis shoes and blue jeans to work that day, and he was up for the challenge as he ran after the would-be robber. Out the front door and into the parking lot they both ran. The robber raced toward another business, determined to get away, but Jonathan increased his speed to another level to close the distance between them.

The robber than turned toward the many houses that were close by, but Jonathan would not give up chase. The robber, clearly exhausted, started to slow down. As Jonathan was closing in on the robber, He said, "Man, you are one of us." Jonathan thought, *No, I am not like you. I do not rob people.* Shortly afterward, Jonathan caught the robber.

Within minutes, the sheriff and deputies showed up and took the young man back to the scene of the crime. Jonathan returned to the store as well and watched as law enforcement officers took witness statements and the attempted robbery reports. Even though the young man tried to fight the law enforcement officers, the ordeal ended peacefully. Jonathan could not have foreseen this coming, but he was glad he'd been able to help.

After that Wednesday morning, things went back to normal. He worked many long hours, and his days off were placed on hold. Jonathan looked forward to the weekend, when he planned to visit his parents. Instead, the assistant manager said that they had to work. Jonathan was disappointed by the news, so he talked with the assistant manager about his plans for the weekend. The discussion got heated, and the assistant manager told Jonathan, "If you can't come to work on Sunday, you might as well say you quit!"

After such negative remark, Jonathan gave the store keys to the assistant manager and walked out the door.

Over next the few days, the news traveled about Jonathan walking off the job. This caused the district manager to get involved, and he reached out to Jonathan, asking for a meeting with him. At the meeting, Jonathan explained in vibrant detail what had happened and how disappointed he was by the outcome. The district manager understood Jonathan's concerns, and in the end, he persuaded Jonathan to return to work.

For several weeks, things went smoothly. Then, one Wednesday morning in late August, Jonathan went in early to open the store. Shortly afterward, he saw the assistant manager. Moments later, the store manager walked into the store. A question crossed Jonathan's mind: *Why do we have three different managers in the store at the same time?*

The answer was about to be revealed. The assistant manager said to Jonathan, "The manager wants to see you."

Without hesitation, Jonathan went to the breakroom and took a seat opposite the store manager, who made his brief announcement: "We are letting you go." The reason he gave for the termination was that Jonathan had a bad attitude, and it was affecting other employees.

Silently, Jonathan exited the store. The news had delivered a powerful emotional punch. It left him speechless.

When he got home, he asked himself, *Where do I go from here?* He had spent more than five years on his first job, and that resulted in his being fired because of lies concocted by someone who did not approve of Jonathan's accomplishments.

Nevertheless, Jonathan knew this was not the end of his story. He was now in the valley, looking toward the many mountain peaks all around him. He told himself, *The only place to go when you are at your lowest is up!* Jonathan knew how to encourage himself.

Jonathan could only go to the mountain peaks. His job was no more, but his faith and hope continued to soar. Jonathan was an ambitious person with a cheerful outlook that would take him to the next level in life. He considered his situation wisely and applied that wisdom to his life. This was not his end; instead, it was a new chapter in his life. He would embrace it with the right attitude and gratitude so that he could fulfill his purpose in life.

CHAPTER 28

◆

Embracing Life's New Normal

There are times when we may feel good about our accomplishments, but we should ask ourselves this question: are we living in God's plans and purpose in our daily living? The year 2020, for many, was a difficult, sad, and chaotic year, where it was nothing close to a 20/20 vision. The vision of clarity and focus did not surface in any way to guide us through such a painful year.

The pain came for many individuals. Whether they were on a mountaintop (rich and famous) or in the valley (poor to middle class), death did not care! Each day, death, sickness, pain, and sorrow continued to rise for man, woman, and child. This crisis was a challenge in ways that we could not imagine, but those of faith continued to press on in Jesus's name.

The next in-an-instant moment was nothing like my previous ones. It was painful and emotional like nothing that most of us had ever seen. It was the year 2020. That year, our normal way of life was turned upside down and inside out; it was filled with a high voltage of chaos. Only the God of creation knows the true outcome of humanity.

Many may have thought that in the year 2020, everything would be seen with much clarity, but it turned into a cloudy, cold, gray, and dark year for most of us. My daily routine shifted from going to work to trying to stay busy every day. I would do the following:

draw, stain wood, make custom picture frames, create wood-burning art, read, and write poetry and songs. I praised God for my many gifts, as one day they will bless others in the name of Jesus Christ, our Savior and King.

Our lives shifted from normal to a challenging day-to-day living. Many worked from home instead of going to the office building. Many lost their jobs, and some companies went out of business. The end result was that many people lived in fear instead of faith in God. Because the pandemic had a powerful grip on the people around the globe, many people lost their homes and lost their loved ones. There were challenges for all of us because the nature of the coronavirus was so severe to the livelihood of humankind. In faith, however, by God's help, I press on, one day at a time.

Millions of people lost their lives and still are dying from COVID-19. We were told to cover our mouths and noses by wearing masks and to stay six feet apart. This was super-hard to do. As human beings, we love to show affection by hugging and kissing.

It was a great challenge, but many took heed of the recommendations from the health professions and doctors to stay safe. This in-an-instant moment caused such chaos, pain, and uncomfortable conditions. Our "normal" living was gone. Also, deep cleaning was recommended to combat the virus.

My situation at work changed from month to month. I would work a month and be off a month. Finally, I spoke with my director to let her know that was not working for me. I gave glory and praise to God because my director understood what I was saying and allowed me to continue to work for the remainder of 2020. There was a total of six weeks when I did not receive any funds on weekly basis, but God supplied our needs.

Many struggled to get food, a safe place to stay, and to pay their bills on time. Many worried about the "normal" that was eroded from their way of living by the dark storm clouds. I was concerned with losing one of my precious normality's that meant so much to me—the normalcy of going to church every week to fellowship with my sisters and brothers in Christ; this was difficult to embrace, but it was part of the new normal. Oh, how I desired for it to end, but it was here to stay for a good while

May God help and be with us all.

The reality of this virus taught me a lesson about being normal. It was a reality check for my spiritual belief because my hope and belief are not embraced by the once normal but instead, by my faith in God. Where does God fit into this crisis equation? Can we go back to being normal in the way we knew it? Can we live our lives normally, when over 5.4 million people have died (according to worldometers.info, as of December 27, 2021)? Has faith in God increased or decreased for humankind?

As a nation, we print on our money, "In God, We Trust." Are we there? Are we even close? Are we trying to do better to get there? Has this virus changed the way we live our lives from day to day? Are we concerned about turning our lives over to the Savior, Jesus Christ? What if this was your last opportunity to do so? Would you, do it? There are so many questions with so few answers.

Nevertheless, I have an answer for you. It is impossible to be normal in the way we once knew it. So many lives have perished, many families are hurting, and many vacancies are on the rise across the globe—vacancies on the job, in the classroom, in the home, in the streets, in the hospital, at the dinner table, and in the bedroom. Therefore, life will never be the same.

Covid-19 caused normalcy to change for all humankind. Many experienced the death of a loved one—young or old, male or female. Many were nurses, doctors, teachers, students, neighbors, spouses, police officers, firefighters, or lawyers. Each of these individuals played a crucial role in the normalcy we once knew. If they are no longer here, then the normal we once knew it does not exist anymore. It is painful and difficult to process in a world filled with sorrow and challenges.

Normalcy has been uprooted and needs to be replanted in new soil. It needs a new vision for the future generations to be more productive for the years to come. We should know one thing about history by now. We cannot change the outcome if we do not change from within ourselves. We cannot do it alone; we need the Savior, Jesus Christ, and the Holy Spirit to help and sustain us. With that in mind, the possibilities have a much greater chance of becoming a reality than we may think.

CHAPTER 29

✦

In-an-Instant Moment

It was a gray, cold, and dark night. Most people were in their beds, fast asleep, hoping to be replenished and rested for the new day to come.

Early on Tuesday morning, December 28, 2021, I awoke at 4:20. The thought crossed my mind to write at that hour of the morning; it was one of my quiet times to do so. Instead, I turned over in bed and went back to sleep.

My in-an-instant moment appeared out of nowhere. I had drifted into a deep sleep, and next thing I knew, I was in a dream—one over which I had no control at that moment. It was frightening to be in a dream that was surreal, bizarre, and strange, all rolled into one.

This is one of the reasons we need to pray and study the Word of God in our faith walk with Jesus Christ. The enemy sits and waits until a vulnerable moment presents itself. It could very well be a drop-of-a-feather moment, slowly twirling toward me, hoping to conquer and defeat my faith in Jesus Christ. In doing so, it causes chaos to my mind, body, and soul. But in God, the power of the Holy Ghost comes to my rescue in my time of need. Take hold, my brothers and sisters. God is still on the throne and in control of the matter at hand. I have faith and continue to trust in Him.

In my dream, I was in my kitchen, preparing breakfast for myself, when I looked out of the window and saw some movement. People appeared to be working. My neighbor had started some carpentry work on my front porch. The right side of the latticed deck had been cut and removed. In the dream, I approached a man who looked like a groundskeeper. He was busy doing the trimming and cutting of bushes and grass.

I asked him about the work being done to my property without my consent. The groundskeeper directed me to my next-door neighbor. Quickly, I turned to that lady to ask, "Who gave you permission to do work on my property?"

She responded, "A man told me to do the work on his property." She didn't know that she was at the wrong address.

I was terribly upset, and in a firm voice, I told her to replace my front deck to the way it was.

How could I allow myself to get this upset about a dream? It had created fear that seemed so real, but the end results were false. This matter was created by the enemy in my vulnerable moment. It was "FEAR"—False Evidence Appearing Real!

That matters because the enemy can attack me in my dreams and cause me to get upset. It matters! I praised God for the Holy Spirit that rests deep within me.

Suddenly, I woke up from my dream and asked God, "Is this what I need to write about?" The answer was yes.

We need to guard our hearts, minds, and souls. We need to pray without ceasing. Prayer changes thing! From where I stand, I see the enemy going into attack mode, trying to conquer our minds, bodies, and souls.

Let tons of praise be offered up to Almighty God, a God who is worthy to be praised. He will find a way for you and me to escape. He is God that sits on His throne in Eternity, and He is always in control.

CHAPTER 30

❖

The Danger That Is upon Us

It was around the early 1990s when the rain started to fall upon the red-clay hills in Georgia. It was around mid-autumn, and changes were taking place—leaves turned color, the temperature got cooler, and harvest time was a beautiful sight to see.

On some farms, however, land was under water. Many roads had water running over them, and the roads and bridges became unsafe because of the swiftly moving water that washed away the dirt from bridges. It was difficult to travel, and driving was extremely dangerous.

I did not know the roads were in such bad condition until I went to visit my parents. I praise God that I made it safely to their home.

On Sunday, the rain stopped, so I made plans to go to church. I knew I would have to travel the longest route to church, so one of my younger sisters decided to go with me. Little did I know that my in-an-instant moment was just a stone's throw away. After church, I decided to take the shortest route back to our parents' house. Was it wise? Probably not.

We had traveled for about two miles when we encountered water on the roadway for about a quarter of a mile. Looking ahead, I saw that I'd also have to drive over a bridge near the boiling spring that was close by. As we approached the bridge, I stopped the car and walked onto the bridge to inspect its safety. As I stood on the bridge,

I saw more than six feet of water twirling beneath the bridge and flowing at a high rate of speed. After inspecting the bridge, I decided that it was safe to cross. Just a fraction of second later, I would have thought differently.

I drove my car slowly across the wooden bridge. As we reached the north side and were on the road again, it happened! A great wall of dirt came crumbling down just after we crossed over the bridge. Now the bridge was impassable because the land on the north side was no longer connected to the bridge; it had washed away into the water. To make matter worse, my car had started to take on water on the inside, and shortly afterward, it stopped running. Now we were stranded in about two feet of water. I knew I had to get my sister, my car, and myself to safety.

Quickly, I rolled up my pant legs, stepped into the water, and raised the hood on my car. After scanning the engine, I saw what had caused the car to stop running. The distributor cap had gotten wet from the water on the roadway. I had to dry it off, but I didn't have a dry cloth. The only way to dry it was to use my socks. Once I did that, I placed the cap back onto the engine distributor.

But that did not solve all the problems. The water needed to be beneath the engine fan, or the same problem would reoccur. The blade design on the fan would pull more water onto the engine on each turn it made.

Next, I pushed the car far enough that the engine fan was above the water. This allowed me to start the engine and drive the car through the water on the road. My sister and I were able to make it to our parents' home, where I then removed the remainder of water from my car. It was a great task, but I was able to accomplish it.

On that day, I learned a great lesson for life: Whenever you see water on the roadway, do not attempt to drive through it! It is too risky and way too dangerous to do so.

On that day, praise God, my sister and I returned safely from church, back to our parents' home.

CHAPTER 31

◆

Gone but Not Forgotten

Perhaps, may be even you can relate to the next in-an-instant moment, but it's very personal to me. It is about loved ones who have gone into eternity.

I think about my dad from time to time and what he means to me. Fond memories have stayed in my mind, and one such memory was from my high school days. My dad was busily at work in his garden before sunrise. As I slowly walked toward him, I felt a peace, like the stillness and freshness of country morning air after a gentle spring rain. It was so real, serene, and clean, like a peace I never had experienced or seen. I had approached him on that morning to ask for some money, and he granted my request.

I miss you, Dad, and I want you to know that this is my tribute to you, wherever I go.

Another fond memory of my dad was when he took two of my younger brothers and me fishing on a hot summer day. He took the time out of his busy workday to spend some quality time with three of his sons. I will not forget, Dad; you may be gone but your legacy lives on in me. I dare to keep these precious memories and not share them with others.

This also is about you, Mom, and the love you gave me when I was little. You cared for me whenever I was sick with a cold, flu, or stomachache. Many times, I needed patches on my blue jeans because I'd worn holes in them. Mom, it was like I was wearing your love anew each time I wore those jeans. You would sew a patch to cover the hole. It was such a warm, loving feeling whenever I put them on to wear again. In the winter months, your loving deed was appreciated even more because my leg and knee were covered from the cold air. Mom, this I will not forget.

You prepared many dinners from scratch and seasoned them in a way only a loving mom would do. I will always remember that, Mom. Today, I bask in the sweet memories of your love, a legacy for generations to read about and to learn the importance of genuine love. This kind of love is needed for humanity. This is my tribute, Mom. I give it to you in love. I dare to keep these precious memories and not share them in love with others.

This is about you, Dorothy—aka, "Dot." I thank you for being my oldest sister; you showed me love in many special ways. You gave of yourself and did not expect anything in return. This is your legacy; your story is positive in every way, helping others to become better people in society. When I was little, I would write letters to you because you were far from home. Since you had a job, I would ask you for money; you honored my request and did not ask for anything in return.

The beautiful expression of love from you, my oldest sister, to one of your much-younger brothers was that you took the time out of your busy day, and you wrote me a letter in return. Also, you showed compassion in your love in ways that were expressed in deeds. Many evenings when we lived in Augusta, Georgia, you would come home from work and prepare hot meals for Mom and me and you. I will never forget the love you showed in special ways like that. This is my tribute to you, Dorothy; I dare to keep these precious memories locked in my heart and mind and not share them with the world around me.

Now it is my next-to-the-baby sister, Leila. We have gone through a lot together. You are one of my special sisters on this side of heaven. You were my traveling sister over the many miles and years we traveled together. You were one of the sisters who kept me informed of the things happening back home when I moved to another state. I thank you for doing that. I miss our lengthy phone calls from time to time. You are deeply missed! This tribute is to you and others. There was one Sunday in the late 1990s when we traveled to Dublin, Georgia, for an evening church service. After the service, we traveled back to Augusta through the towns of Sandersville, Louisville, and Wrens, Georgia. Then, the unexpected happened, without any warning.

Out of the beautiful sunset on a sizzling summer evening, a sheriff's deputy appeared and decided to pull us over. Only God truly knows why, but he followed us for numerous miles before pulling us over. I stopped and waited for him to approach my car and ask for my driver's license and registration. He did, and I complied and waited. The deputy returned to his vehicle. About twenty minutes later, he returned to my car and gave me my license. Shortly afterward, we were on our way home, where we enjoyed one of the many joyful Sunday dinners we had. We ate together, along with our niece and her mom, our baby sister. Leila, you are missed! This is my tribute to you because of the love you showed to others and me when you were on this earth. I want to thank you for being there, time after time. I dare to keep such joyful memories bottled in my mind and heart. I must share them with the world to enrich the lives of humankind.

This is my tribute to all of you in love, until we reach our eternal place of rest in heaven above.

CHAPTER 32

◆

A Message Made Plain

Sometimes, life sends profound messages. As human beings, we may fail to humble ourselves to comprehend the message in time to apply it to our lives. If we see things changing for the worst, do we stand our ground to survive? Does our faith take on greater hope and flourish to the finish line called eternity?

This is the world in which we live with in-an-instant moments. It is the searchlight and not the spotlight. When an object is already the spotlight, there is a greater need to become the searchlight. It is called a sign of the times. Look at the world we live in. Here are some of those spotlights:

Deep in the ocean, a formidable power is released by a volcano or an earthquake into tons of water that cause a tsunami and a mighty flood. This should cause humankind to seek the face of almighty God. The power of many ferocious tornadoes, clearing a path for hundreds of miles, descending a wrath like no humans have ever seen in their lifetimes. This should cause all humanity to take notes and run into the presence of almighty God.

We have seen blistering fires raging, like they are from a burning hell, creating an inferno of destruction on trees and property in its path, as far as the eyes can see.

We see numerous males and females choosing to live together instead of being married and committed to their spouses. The love of many has waned and turned cold like subzero temperatures. Yet these are some of the serious matters that need to be told. It is for our eternal souls. May this behoove all humankind to seek God's face while He can be found.

The COVID-19 crisis has reached the shores of more than two years and still has destructive power to spare. Humankind no longer needs this type of pain, where we cannot gain. We are living lives of sorrow, and we decree, in Christ Jesus, that this crisis one day will no longer remain. Our prayers to seek almighty God will be heard. Then, an internal change will take place and change the lives of the people. It can take place in a powerful, profound way. The key for this to happen is found in the Bible:

> If my people which are called by my name, shall humble themselves and pray, and seek my face and turn from their wicked ways; then will I hear from Heaven and forgive them their sin and will heal their land. (2 Chronicles 7:14 KJV)

Yes, Lord Jesus, our land needs to be healed.

CHAPTER 33

◆

Peace, Miracle, and Praise Moments

As human beings, we search for peace, but we do not find it. This is because the places or things for which we are searching are wrong. Real peace can only come from God because we belong to Him. He made us in His likeness, according to the first chapter of Genesis.

I encountered earthly peace, however, in a forest on a late fall evening, while walking along the creek banks. It was the sound of the running water, flowing slowly in the creek from an everlasting boiling spring. The water cascaded off the small rocks and fallen limbs, positioned at the right angle to create soft music like nothing I'd ever heard. This was profound peace on earth to embrace in my lifetime.

Joyfully, I continued my walk in the forest among hundreds of trees. I paused for a moment to listen to the many leaves as they tumbled and twirled across the earth floor. They created a soft, musical sound with the help of the Master of Creation's touch. The gentle wind produced music for the divine ears to hear at a precise time and place.

When you have experienced peace like that, the chaos of this world cannot touch it, no matter how difficult life on earth may be. It is joy—boundless joy—to know the peace of God for yourself, every day.

This next in-an-instant moment and the way I experienced it is nothing less than a miracle

It is joyous and refreshing to grow up on a farm in the country. My siblings and I had the opportunity to experience it. We had many responsibilities, such as feeding the animals and harvesting food for them, gathering wood for the home, and completing my schoolwork assignments. Country living was a great part of my life that I won't forget. It keeps me humble and balanced each day.

It was not just all about work, though. There were many games to play—hopscotch, dodgeball, softball, and basketball, as well as tossing a Frisbee. There was more than enough to keep my siblings and me busy on the farm.

Here is an in-an-instant moment from the late 1970s. My siblings and I had returned home from school. As I stepped off the school bus, I noticed the firewood was getting low in the woodpile. I knew what my job for the evening was—to cut a load of firewood. It was late fall, and the days were shorter, so I knew I had to move quickly to cut the firewood before it got dark. I quickly changed out of my school clothes and into my farm clothes. I gathered the chainsaw, ax, gas, and oil to put in my daddy's pickup, and off I drove to cut the firewood.

Once I was in the woods, I scanned the forest for oak trees, for one that would produce a quick load of firewood. I spotted a tall one with limbs at the very top of the tree and about fifteen inches in diameter. I grabbed the chainsaw, ax, gas, and oil and walked toward the tree.

My daddy taught me to decide beforehand which direction to allow the tree to fall to the ground. For safety, it was best to try to prevent it from falling onto other trees. It was extremely dangerous if that happened. The reason was that it would be too difficult and dangerous to cut a tree that was hanging on the limbs of another tree. The limbs on the other tree could give way without warning or they can break under the dead weight of the tree at a moment notice.

So, I checked the wind direction—another factor to consider, as the wind can blow the tree back onto the unaware chainsaw operator.

After the many safety checks, I was good to go. Little did I know, a miracle was about to happen. I started the chainsaw and started to cut the oak tree. I cut a plug out of the tree on the opposite side, in the direction I wanted it to fall. As I was cutting, while watching the top of the tree to see which way it was about to fall, I made an overcut of the tree—I had cut the tree completely off the stump. Then, it happened in an instant!

The tree did a counterclockwise turn, rolled off the stump, and landed vertical on the ground, taking the chainsaw with the tree. The amazing thing about this was that I was using a bow chainsaw, and the tree was standing vertical inside the bow of the saw. I stood in awe, amazed at what happened before my eyes. There was no way to cut the tree down or to get the chainsaw unbound from the tree.

After that, I cannot explain what took place. The last thing I recall, I was staring at the oak tree and thinking, *What can I do to get the tree on the ground?*

Even now, I cannot recall what happened after that incident. And it puzzles me each time I think about it. But I do recall the load of wood being on my dad's pickup, and by first dark, I was driving the truck home, with no injuries or damages to the pickup or to me. Praise be to God! This may seem impossible, but I must disagree. Because I am a man of faith, I do believe in miracles.

It is a blessing to know that there are divine interventions out there somewhere when we need them the most. I can't explain it, but the Holy Bible speaks of entertaining strangers, unaware of who they may be.

> Be not forgetful to entertain strangers; For, thereby some have entertained angels unawares. (Hebrew 13:2 KJV)

On that day, among the thick forest of trees, something miraculous took place. Divine intervention took place at the appropriate time, according to God's purpose, plan, and will.

Take time to find your purpose in this world and go to the place where it is needed the most. Amen

My next in-an-instant moment is unique in every way. In the late 1980s, I received a phone call from my mom, telling me that one of her brothers had died. She needed me to take her to the funeral. I made plans to drive to Savannah, Georgia by renting a mid-size Tahoe SUV to drive to the funeral.

On a wet Saturday morning, the day of the funeral, I left Augusta early, before sunrise, to pick up my mom and one of my brothers. As I was traveling in the dark on Highway 305, a large tree appeared, in an instant, across the roadway. Somehow, I was able to maneuver around it without turning the SUV over or hitting or running over the tree. I do not know how I did it, but God does. I am a man of faith who believes in miracles.

As I continued my drive in the dark morning hours, I came upon an emergency maintenance building. I stopped to tell the person on duty about the fallen tree that was covering the roadway and then was on the road once again.

When I reached my parents' home and went inside the house, my mom asked me, "What is the matter?"

I assumed that I must look frightened about something—she was able to see it without me revealing anything to her. It could have been that my maneuvering the SUV earlier had frightened me more than I realized. But praise God, I was OK.

After a moment, I composed myself, and soon afterward we got on road, traveling to Savannah. We had a safe trip there and back, and nothing happening to the SUV at all. Later that day, I was on the road, back to Augusta. I praised God for a safe return home.

CHAPTER 34

◆

The Power of Endurance

It is painful to see the destructive impact of the COVID-19 crisis. People have suffered and have fought to breathe to stay alive in many places around the world. It is difficult to comprehend what is taking place in society with family and loved ones. All survivors are welcome to the table because of their endurance and strength for the soul of humankind and to encourage and support each individual in his or her spiritual journey.

Many may feel that this is the worst thing a human being could encounter, but there is good news even in the worst of storms. The good I saw in this, from my perspective, was that God kept me working safely, most of the time. He provided for my family and me during this crisis. I must give God the praise, glory, and honor for His faithfulness, day after day. My hope for this to be better, over with, finished, and never to raise its ugly head again.

We must have an enduring spirit on this earthly journey. This enduring spirit is not a physical aspect that you and I can see. It is connected to the spiritual realm that enhances the physical body to be a better individual in society. It behooves all of us to endure this, to finish strong in the faith race. We need this endurance power!

In 2018, I wrote the following words:

Endurance Prayer

Oh, heavenly Father of creation and life, You are omnipotent. Grant unto me the power I need for each day. The power to be spiritual, physical, mental, financial, social, and emotional is part of my daily need. May it be a witness to others each day.

Dear heavenly Father, grant me the words to say and when and how to say them. Let my words be a beacon of hope as a witness to humankind in love. And for every action I encounter, grant me the right reaction. May the glory, honor, and praise return unto You in the most holy and powerful name of Jesus Christ, our Lord. Amen.

The year 2020 also displayed hatred by others, causing chaos for humankind. Some appeared to be concerned about the number of people who died from the virus, but on the other hand as they expressed hate (being disrespectful and wanting to fight others about their choice to get vaccinated or wear a mask for protection), which caused chaos to escalate only to deter others from doing the right thing. Is this not living a double standard?

I get it! This virus kills! One's age, color, looks, or the standard of living is not a concern. Hate is as deadly. It attacks at any time in places where many dead bodies are left behind. This is as bad or worse as the virus itself because the result is still death.

Many have suffered and died because of hate. The level of hate is increasing in the world, but thanks be to God for His Word! This is not the end of the story. The power of hate was defeated in the battle at Calvary. Jesus Christ died for the sins of humankind. And it did not end there. He rose on the third day to set humankind free. The eternal and loving God, the Creator of life did this for humankind, not for some but all humanity. In spite of our shortcomings and sin, He still loves humankind unconditionally.

It is agape love that no amount of money can purchase. No one else can produce it or could duplicate it. The God of creation already knew it. So, He sent Jesus Christ to live and prove it. This only happened so we could believe and receive Him.

I saw lives changed before my eyes, some for the good and some for bad. On the spectrum for good, many people gave their lives to God, and many rededicated their lives back to Him.

It is a good feeling to know in whom you place your trust until life ends on this earth. I know where I place my faith; it is in God 'til life ends. Many individuals have given of their time, money, and selves in a selfless way. I do praise God for the good in people because when it comes to helping others, there is something in our DNA that comes to the forefront of our lives in love. This is powerful, beautiful and a remarkable sight to be seen through the eyes of humanity in love.

This next in-an-instant moment happened on February 23, 2022, at 4:45 a.m. It is something I wrote, and I give the praise and glory to God for allowing me to write as often as he gives me the words, stories, and design to create in the early morning hours.

I Shall Be Free

I shall be free from this world of pain.
Help me to stay focus and not be ashamed.
May the life I live will be a blessing to others and a powerful
    gain.
Keep faith anchored ever so close in my soul.
This I know from the words of the Holy Bible and the days
    of old.
You are my Savior I love the most.
Keep me strong by keeping me close.
I soon will be free from this world of great misery.
There is sorrow great and wide.
It brings many teardrops to my eyes.
Help me to not lose control

From when I am young until the day, I am old.

When days come and I feel I cannot cope,

Increase my power of faith, built on You, my God, an everlasting
hope.

I shall be free from this world of such misery.

I do not know where else to turn.

You are the one I need the most, when in life, I have become
overwhelmed with deep concern.

There is no other peaceful place I can go.

I thank Jesus Christ for blessing me so,

To author these words, so others may know.

Keep me strong so I can journey on,

For it only takes a twinkle of an eye, and we all could be gone.

Finally, in eternity, our eternal home.

Then I will be free from this world of great misery.

CHAPTER 35

◆

Hate, Love, Eternity

As of this writing, it has been around eleven days since the war in Ukraine started. There has been pain, chaos, death, bloodshed, and evil acts by selfish human beings, compelled by sin and hate. I have seen lives changed in an instant like I have never seen in my decades of living. Loved ones have been killed and families broken and separated from one another by such odious acts of hatred. That is war; it is hatred in the heart of humankind in the worst ways. This is being done to another human being.

The world in which we live is surrounded by evil. It appears that goodness has packed its bags and gone to an unknown place. The lives of humanity are driven by love. It is our love and desire to do this or that. The sad reality is that many define love in a wrongful and sinful way. Love is pure when it is for the common good to humanity. It can be in various deeds that build and encourage the heart of humankind.

Many people have money, but the love of it is a sin. When people love money, they will do just about anything to get it. The Bible speaks of this:

> For the love of money is a root of all kinds of evil,
> for which some have strayed from the faith, in their

greediness, and pierced themselves through with many sorrows. (1 Timothy 6:10 KJV)

In other words, you cannot love money and not have sorrows follow whatever you are lusting after. This is the reasons why I put pen to paper—so others can know and understand, and God gets the glory. With this war between Russia and Ukraine, not one human being should see the impact of the war and not have their emotions stirred in an uncomfortable way. The measurement of the stirring should be enough to make individuals take a stand for what is right and to show love to all humankind. I am in. How about you?

The power of hate is deadly, and it can kill at a moment's notice. It will not stop at anything, other than love—the agape love of God. The question is, what can defeat and defuse such hate? It is love, the love of the Savior, Jesus Christ. He died for the sins of humankind. Hate was defeated at Calvary, and nothing and no person can change that. Today, when one is in Christ Jesus, there is no need to live in fear. There is a scripture in the Holy Bible that reads, "Therefore to him that knoweth to do good, and doeth it not, to him it is sin" (James 4:17 KJV). This lets me know that within my power, I have the authority to do good. Whenever the opportunity presents itself, I know to act and fulfill the good requested in James 4:17.

This is agape love at the greatest you will ever know. This love is not physical or materialistic; it's not for individuals to choose as they desire. Instead, it is for those who decide to accept, believe, and confess their sins, acknowledging Jesus Christ as their personal Savior. Our Lord and Savior, Jesus Christ, still loves us, even when we feel like we are not worthy of being loved. He died for all humankind, not just some of humankind.

This war touched a nerve deep within my being. I cannot be idle, neutral, or crippled to this hateful act by humankind to other human beings. This hate is seen around the world. It is against humanity in the worst way possible. Some people are greedy and selfish toward others of the same stature. An attitude like that fuels the hate deep within oneself. We are not any different in the eyes of God. I must express my voice against such hatred toward humankind on every platform that is known to society.

It concerns me when I see innocent lives being killed—all age groups, male and female. These people want to live. All they want to do is escape from harm's way and be at liberty to make choices for themselves. They no longer want to be oppressed and live their lives in fear. A life not free is a life locked or chained, with restrictions enforced by an evil power, known as dictatorship. The nerve of telling one what to do, when to do it, and how to do it; it's like each individual cannot speak or do for themselves. This is not what humanity is about or truly needs. Humanity needs the Salvation of Jesus Christ in order to be free. By God's help, I will continue to write these words as long as I am blessed and alive.

Let us take the stand in unity. We have the power to bring about real change. Hate must pack its things and leave for an eternal destination into the unknown. Hate, you are no longer welcome here in this place of peace. You have created too much chaos, sorrow, and pain. You are never to return again. The people have spoken, and the verdict is in; it is final. This case is closed. A change is coming on the horizon, and it is forever near. Hate can no longer stay here.

The people have taken a stand against hate and wars all around the world. The people want more out of life. By now, hate is confused from such an outpouring of unity by the people. The force of hate tries to move against love with wars and disagreements toward peaceful and loving humankind. Love changes each individual from the inside to the outside to be productive in society every day in every way.

I am reminded of words spoken by a wise man. He said, "Before one sets out to build, one must count the cost." I say to leadership and those in authority, before you display hate against another human being, you need to count the cost. There is a price to be paid on many levels as one journeys on this path called hate! This price carries no value but much weight—the price of material things, loved one's lives, jobs, homes, cars, families, and even a personal price; the loss of one's soul if one does not accept, believe, and confess that

Jesus Christ is Lord. What will it cost you, my brothers and sisters, if you humble yourself before God, family, neighbors, and fellow human beings? The choice is yours. Which one will you choose: love or hate? Think on these words, my fellow humans, and rise to take a stand for what is true and right for life on earth, for all humankind.

In contrast, on the spectrum for bad, many lives were lost around the world. The people we once knew are now a memory. These individuals may be gone but are not forgotten.

There were many other bad circumstances to deal with. Many killings and shootings started to escalate in various cities across this country. The sad part about it is, many of the shootings happened in the daytime, and the lives of loved ones were taken in a hateful or undeserved way. Many were at jobs, in neighborhoods, at businesses, and in other places across this beautiful country. My fellow neighbors, where did we go wrong? This crisis is like a war that we cannot win on our own, but the impact from it is devastation to humanity in the worst way possible.

CHAPTER 36

◆

The Price of War

On Tuesday, March 15, 2022, I awoke at 2:50 a.m. The subject of war on my mind compels me to continue to write about it.

As of this writing, it is the third week of fighting the war in Ukraine. It seems so insane; the people are praying for a peaceful change, hoping this war will not remain. My question is this: what is the enemy hoping to gain? The war has caused death, bloodshed, sorrow, money, heartache, tearstained eyes, hate, and pain.

War is inevitable, and God knows it will be. He has known the heart of humankind from the beginning. Without God, humankind will become like a desert. God knows sin will raise its ugly head and create chaos, pain, sorrow, and death, and humankind needs to be set free from it. When one is not free, one is like an egg placed in a microwave, waiting for the precise moment to explode. It is vital that each second is taken into consideration to save the egg. Likewise, each second of every minute should be taken into consideration in saving the soul and life of each individual at risk in this war.

Humankind is born into a world of sin. God knows the route we will take in life and the time we will take it. Mostly, it is the route where we do not depend on Him, but God still loves and cares for us. As human beings, we think we can survive on our own, but the evidence says differently. We cannot do it on our own! We need God's amazing grace and love to be at peace and filled with happiness in this world.

The only way to get there from where you stand is through His only begotten Son, Jesus Christ. The question is, will you choose Him today and be filled with the Holy Ghost? I have seen on the news, day after day, the bloodshed, lives perished, and hope and dreams faded in this war in Ukraine. This crisis is painful to watch as the world sees innocent lives being killed and places where people once lived made unlivable and destroyed by hate. What is this war about? Is it about regions or land?

After a person dies, there is no U-Haul following behind the hearse to the grave. We bring nothing into this world, and we carry nothing when we leave it. Do not become too attached to this world; it is not our home,

Whenever I see a war, two major factors come to mind. The Holy Bible speaks of it when the sign of the time comes. This lets me know that war is inevitable. In Matthew 24:1–51, the sign is shared with much light on the subject. One key verse to focus on is Matthew 24:6. It speaks of war and rumors of wars. I am a born-again child of God. I see the Holy Bible being revealed and fulfilled at this level. I must take note and stand firm in my faith every day so I can endure until the end.

The endurance of the people is seen as a witness from abroad. They are determined to take a stand for what is right—for all people, not just some people. To have faith and take a stand for what is right is rewarding in itself. It appears to me that the faith of the Ukrainians is stronger than any war they are fighting at this time. It is seen in the resilience and determination to fight for such freedom. It is so sad to see so many people waste time and energy on material things that are temporary to all of humanity.

Again, we are born with nothing, and we leave the world with nothing. The question is, why are people fighting and killing over something that does not belong to humanity in the first place? Everything belongs to God. He can do as He pleases. We are just stewards over things while we are here on this earth.

All hope is not gone. When one is in Christ Jesus, there is an eternal hope that shines brighter than what the natural eyes can see. This is the reason we need faith because in faith, the natural is no more. Spiritual comes to the forefront. Our eternal souls will live as long as God shall live. He made this possible when He created man and breathed life into his lungs. Then man became a living soul. The book of Genesis says it best. Take some time and read it for yourself.

The price for war is out of reach for humankind to survive on its own. It will take the agape love of God, the Father; Jesus Christ, the Begotten Son, and the Holy Ghost to make the three in one. The eternal spirit of the Holy Ghost, to sustain us to live in this world of sin, is very much needed. Without Him, no human being can win in this world filled with unlimited sin, and no one can live in it without God's help. My prayer to you is this: take a moment to decide for yourself. Which route will you take? Will it be the Holy Bible? Or will it be your way, the self-taught way? A life of sin is a sure way for you to never win. The choice is yours. Use wisdom because your choice will become a permanent one from now into eternity.

CHAPTER 37

◆

The War Cry I See

At 3:04 a.m. on March 21, 2022, I was awakened once again from a deep sleep. In my spirit, I felt compelled to write the following valuable and compassionate words:

In this war, I see pain, suffering, and deaths of loved ones. This war cry of sorrows can be seen by many of the bodies of humanity lying in the streets. Many people are taking a stand and being courageous individuals, willing to fight for freedom, even if it means going down in defeat. It is difficult to hear the war cry that is made by the people who are willing to fight for families and the lives of future generations.

The war cry of many babies is heard loud and clear because they do not have the strength or the ability to defend themselves. Their lives were shattered but not in vain, for the perishing of each precious life still has a purpose, and each life's purpose will cause humankind to change. The people with tearstained eyes started to swell with sorrow, and the hope within has increased their faith. They trust and believe in God Almighty that all is well. This is the war cry I see.

This is the people's desire, filled with freedom fire. It is the desire by the people who want to be free from a life of oppression, pain, and misery. In contrast, I see the people saying, in their actions and less in words, "Grant me liberty or grant me death." A choice for all humanity is to encourage the people with the importance of freedom. They are willing to sacrifice their lives for the love of God, families, and country. This is the war cry I see.

Hate and war go hand in hand; their shady foundation is sin. One of the sad, horrific moments for me was the bombing of a building. The courageous men and women who were first responders went into action. They rushed into a building that had just been bombed. They did not know what the outcome would be. In midst of all the bombing and chaos, this team was able to rescue a pregnant woman. I watched in sorrow and then was elated with joy at the same time when she was rescued. My love for her leaped within the wall of my being. The news was beautiful, but I later found out that the pregnant woman did not make it. She and her unborn baby both died. This is the price for war. Let's wise up and do better so we can be better. Many questions come to mind. Who was this woman? Was she married? Did she have any children? Are her parents still living?

When I think about war, the image that comes to mind is selfish feeding by dining off sin. It does not matter who loses or wins. War is inevitable in this world of sin. What human beings can be so full of themselves and go to such a low as this yet think that repercussions will not come to them? It is The Agape Love that is missing from their lives. The only way a change will come for each individual is if a miracle takes place. God will have to change them from the inside out. Then, the Holy Spirit will take charge and fill them with Agape Love. This is the answer to the people, that good can come in the midst of most wars. It is only God of creation who can do this for humanity every day.

The eyes of the people are open, and now they can see.

On Saturday, March 19, 2022, I was up early, around 5:10 a.m. As for this writing, the war in Ukraine is raging at a greater level than what humanity ever imagine it would be; it is very painful to watch. All of us surely have stirred emotions deep within and want to help. The death, chaos, fire, hate, and anger are still raging like wildfire feeding on a pile of dry forest underbrush.

This war is senseless in every way. The question is, does it make sense for a country to attack their own citizens and destroy cities, material things, and buildings that made the country what it was, before the war started? Does it make sense to kill innocent lives when they are too young to defend for themselves? My answer is absolutely, no! When will this stop? The answer is, when Jesus Christ returns for His children to take them home to eternity to live with Him forever.

The children, men, and women are willing to fight for their lives, freedom, and country, even when they are afraid of the outcome. They are courageous in their fight to the very end. Some things to consider: what if the very people who are killed have the cure for cancer? What if they have a new and safer way to combat the diseases that are taking innocent lives all across the globe? What about the cure for COVID-19?

My advice for you is to inhale and then exhale. How did that feel? The air you and I breathe is not ours alone. It belongs to a loving, caring God who loves us in spite of our sins and shortcomings. No one is perfect in this world. What are you doing with the air you breathe to stay alive? Are you doing good or evil? The choice is yours. Choose it wisely.

What goes up will come down. On this early Sunday morning, March 27, 2022, it is noticeably quiet, and I can feel the presence of peace deep within my soul. The following is my in-an-instant moment: It took place several years ago, but I remember it like it was yesterday. I was reflecting over my life, and I noticed how good God had been to me.

I thanked God for my dad and his wisdom, teachings, and training that he gave me over many years. I thought about guns and the importance of respecting any gun as if it is loaded at all times. My dad taught me how to carry a loaded gun. He taught me how to load and unload a gun. He taught me never to point a loaded gun toward myself or anyone else. He taught me to always unload the gun before entering the house or getting into a vehicle before driving.

With today's shootings going on, a number of people do not respect guns or to learn about safety for themselves and others.

Several years ago in Ohio, early on a Sunday morning, my family and I went to church. It was quiet and peaceful as I listened to the sound of the birds singing in the trees. In the past, I had backed my car into the driveway numerous times, and I had done so the night before. Something, however, on that particular Sunday morning took place in a miraculous way. I returned from church and backed my car into the driveway as I normally did. That Sunday seemed no different from any other. I went in the house to change my clothes. But this Sunday, it *was* different! I had gone in the house but returned to retrieve something from my car, parked in the driveway.

There it was—a round, black object embedded into the driveway's asphalt. I walked closer to get a good look—and it was a bullet! It had landed just a few inches from my car's gas tank. Only God knows what would have happened if I was parked in the driveway when the bullet landed in the asphalt.

My advice to humankind, be kind to yourself and others as you travel your life journey day by day. It is crucial to respect and be safe with all guns, whether loaded or unloaded.

Today, in the city I live in and around the globe, guns are a major problem. Many people fire their guns into the unknown, not thinking of the impact that bullet will have when it lands. Another word of advice, please be considerate of others in all things. Consider others more than yourself. Do it as if someone's life depends on it. It does!

This world is suffering in numerous ways, which compelled me to write the following lines to a song:

Agape Love for Humanity

Agape love is what the people in this world need.
The heart of humankind is still within a void so deep, yet many people still do not believe.

It is agape love for you and me, like it should be.

Many people are searching to find true love that is kind, and they still cannot see.

All they need to embrace is the agape love that is divine.

It is compassionate love for humankind.

This we need to do while there is still time.

In a humble way, it will be kind.

The people need to ask our Heavenly Father for forgiveness and pray.

He is our sublime; it is true; I hope you do not mind.

It is His power of agape love that causes humankind to stay and not stray.

This is the plan by the Creator of Life; It is like the melody in a song being played in a compassionate way.

Agape love in every day is the ultimate way for all humankind to heal.

This is one true spiritual way that one must tell it in order for it to be revealed.

CHAPTER 38

◆◈◆

There Are Thieves among Us

This in-an-instant moment is a true invention story; the names and places have changed. The story involves the loss of funds by individuals dealing with a scam company. You may be able to relate to something similar. We need to be more aware and alert to such crime taking place in our backyards. We need to combat the problem and display it before it spirals out of control in our communities, cities, and states. Justice is still waiting to serve those involved in such mean and selfish acts toward humankind.

In the little town of Oak Central, USA, there once were three determined, ambitious, young black men, wanting to do something unique and personal. What they had in mind would revolutionize landscaping on the home front and for major businesses. It would be a blessing to all humankind in a special and powerful way.

These three black men were brothers. MC, the inventor, was busy working on his new invention in his parents' car shed. He had worked on his invention for most of the summer, almost every day. One day, he felt confident enough to take the next step in his battery-operated lawn mower invention. MC shared with his brother what he had invented. All the components were in place, ready to go to the next level. MC showed one of his younger brothers, IC3, the artist/designer, the benefits of a battery-powered lawn mower. Some of those benefits were: no need for an extension cord, no need for oil and gas. This would save the consumers money when mowing the lawn. It would be more environmentally safe as well.

One day, MC was in the car shed when IC3 dropped in for a visit. IC3 looked at the prototype as MC explained it to him, and he liked what he was hearing. They had been close brothers for many years. MC was proud and happy about his invention. He explained all the details about the battery-powered lawnmower in every way a potential owner might desire to know about it. After sharing his invention with IC3, MC asked IC3 to draw the lawn mower for him. This was one of the next levels to which MC wanted to go. IC3 agreed to do the drawing.

MC knew that he would need an investor to take this project to the next level, and the person he had in mind was one of his older brothers, JC. However, before JC, the investor, would come on board, he wanted to see a drawing of the battery-powered lawn mower. That motivated IC3 to get busy with the drawing for MC's new invention.

After couple of hours, IC3 had finished the drawing. He showed it to MC, and MC was incredibly pleased. Later during that same week, MC reached out to JC about his new project's drawing. After a short meeting, strategizing their next move, MC and JC agreed to drive to Capitol Ville, USA.

Early the following week, MC and JC drove several miles to the city of Capitol Ville. As they arrived in the city, they saw a sign that read, "Be an inventor who develops your idea or invention into a finished product as you desire it to be. Let our company, Bright Ideas, LLC, assist you in fulfilling your dream."

Things were changing and moving fast for these young black men. Once MC and JC found the street address, they parked their vehicle and walked to the front entrance of the building. The secretary greeted them, and afterward, they made their way to the sixteenth-floor office. MC and JC had already scheduled a meeting with the chief engineer of the New Invention team.

After all the attendees arrived, the meet-and-greet took place.

Afterward the greetings, the meeting started. The important business aspects of the invention were discussed, along with various details and what it would take for an invention to become a reality. After about ninety minutes, the meeting was adjourned. The chief engineer discussed the next step to which MC and JC should take their invention project. There was a cost to advance to the next level, which was reaching out to various companies about their unique invention. For MC and JC, everything was looking very promising. The cost was to be paid bimonthly until paid in full.

So, JC did his part and invested in the project, BLM (Battery Lawn Mower). Things were coming together in a positive way. JC was determined to see project BLM through to completion. Even though everything was looking positive, however, there was one incident that puzzled JC.

During the meeting, JC noticed that there were other inventors in the same meeting, talking about their own inventions. JC wondered why all of the inventors were in the same meeting at the same time, discussing their own inventions in the presence of other inventors. Was it wise to do that and still be discreet about each inventor's invention? Little did JC, MC, and the rest of the inventors know what was about to take place. This company was about to steal invention(s) from the very people who were at the meeting, trying to learn the next step for their inventions. There were some payments made to help the chief engineer to take each invention to the next level. JC did his part and tried to stay positive, but he felt some uneasiness.

After the meeting, JC and MC were looking forward to the next stage of their invention project. JC continued his payments to Bright Ideas, LLC, as often as he could, until one day, he decided to call the company. He dialed the number, but no one answered. JC thought maybe they were busy, and he decided to call at another time.

On the following day, he called again; no one answered. Finally, one day, he called and received a disappointing message: *This number is no longer in service.* JC had now received the answer to his uneasiness. Oh, how gullible JC felt and so disappointed. It was plain and simple: theft had taken place with the company and stole the inventions and the funds that were paid. And they seemed to have disappeared into thin air.

As consumers, we need to be alert and aware of this type of fraudulent activity. It can cripple the growth process in any city that is trying to do what is right in an honest way. Protocol needs to be in place when the consumers, as inventors, try to make their inventions a reality. One protocol is having your idea patented or copyrighted before sharing it with someone outside the invention team. Protocols that *should* be in place include (1) make copies of your ideas, (2) save all receipts, and (3) if funds are exchanged, be sure to get a receipt with the company's name, and make sure someone signs the receipt in person.

Also, do some research about the company with which you are about to do business. Can anyone vouch for this company or business? How long has the company been in business? Has anyone filed complaints against the company? If so, what are they? These are some of the preventive measures that we, as consumers, can take to be safe and aware when doing business with a company.

The fraudulent company was investigated. Some of the funds were returned to the investors and inventors from a legal matter perspective.

Fast-forward about twenty years later, these are the questions that come to IC3's mind: Why bring a volume of products to market at this time? Why was this not done when the theft took place? Could it have been a cooling-off period to let things quiet down before going to the production phase of project BLM? This way it would be less noticeable after so many years had passed. However, IC3 was always on the lookout for various products on the retail market, and sure enough, these products hit the retail space in various entities. Could it be that the theft that was done on false pretenses had started to reap the benefits from production of the battery products for sale?

Since the deception, IC3 has seen numerous products that are using a battery system to operate. They can be found in various hardware stores and retail stores. This started many years ago when three young black men decided to create a battery-operated lawn mower. The lawn mower that IC3 drew many years ago has some of the same visual representations as those on the market today.

The persons who committed such an egregious act in stealing other people's work (inventor, investor, and artist) will one day answer for their actions.

CHAPTER 39

◆

There Is Lawlessness in the Land

In today's society, one's story needs to be told. The information in that story might prevent another human being from becoming the victim of fraud. There are many types of fraud that target older citizens. Scammers think the elderly are easy prey and more vulnerable because of their age. Please, my fellow humans, be safe out there! The elderly also appears to have more money that scammers can steal, but I am here to tell you differently. How do I know this to be true? Because I am close to that age group.

Please, madam and sir, do not fall for phone fraud. Hang up the phone immediately! Get informed on this subject. Educate yourself with knowledge on this egregious act. The law of the land and the commandment of the Holy Bible do not appear to be taken into consideration as we live our lives around one another. Does it matter? Yes, it does matter if you are a born-again child of God. As human beings, we live in this world, but it is not our eternal home. I have seen the law of the land and commandments of the Holy Bible disregarded in many ways. Here are some of those ways:

On my way to work one morning, I had a frightening in-an-instant moment. Because I live nearly twenty miles from my workplace, I try to leave for work early so I will not be late. On this morning, I was traveling north on the east side of Columbus, Ohio. I was in the inside lane, traveling toward the Columbus exit. Just as

I approached the first incline, a four-wheel-drive pickup came out of the darkness and decided to pass me on my left side, driving in the emergency lane at a high rate of speed. He did not respect the laws for driving or the safety of other drivers on the interstate. But praise God for His protection over and around me on that day, as He kept me safe from afar.

The highways are more dangerous than I have ever seen. I have seen mattresses, chairs, parts of vehicles (bumper and tires), dead animals, and other debris on and beside the highway. These are safety hazards to the drivers. The safety of each driver is the responsibility of all drivers on the highways, freeways, and roadways; they should do their parts in being courteous to all drivers.

I am reminded of 2 Thessalonians 2:7, which reads:

> For the mystery of iniquity doth already work only he who now letteth will let, until he be taken out of the way.

This type of lawlessness is seen in many ways. I see it in people who are driving. I have seen drivers driving without headlights on, even when it is dark. I have seen drivers not stop for stop signs and red lights. Is it because they are distracted by something in their vehicle, or is it careless actions on their part?

Another in-an-instant moment occurred in the first week in May 2022 in Reynoldsburg, Ohio. It was foggy that morning. I had driven onto the main street that connected to a busy freeway on my way to work. I stopped my car at a stop sign. I looked to my right (the light was red) and then left (a vehicle was coming). As I looked to my right a second time, the light was still red. Slowly, I made a right turn, barely rolling toward the traffic and the traffic light in front of me.

Without any warning, the coming vehicle passed me on the wrong side of the road, quickly the driver cut across in front of my vehicle without signaling and stopped. The pickup driver only had a few seconds to spare before he would have had a major rear-end collision. He barely missed my car and the vehicle in front of his pickup.

Many times, when we are driving, we get distracted by something or someone in our vehicle. It could be the radio, cell phone, or eating food. It only takes a moment, and many lives can be changed from a positive to a negative. It can be a final result filled with pain and sorry, with no hope in their spirit to see a brighter tomorrow. It could even cause death from a crash. We have to do better, to be able to see and be better, as we drive to and from our destination. Here is *Food for Thought*, we as drivers have our destination to get to, with some kindness and courtesy, by God's Gray and Mercy, we will get there safely.

After nearly causing a rear-end accident, the driver continued in his aggressive and careless driving. After driving for few yards, he changed lanes without signaling again and then immediately cut back in front of me, which nearly caused an accident. He then quickly turned onto another road and drove away. But I did get his license plate number for the record. He was the type of driver who needed a redo in driver's education.

My next in-an-instant moment happened on Mother's Day 2022. I was taking my youngest daughter to work just before 8:00 a.m. As we were traveling through the neighborhood, a pickup made an illegal turn onto my side of the street, heading straight toward my vehicle. Praise God, I was watching where I was driving. I had to apply my brakes and horn so we would not collide head-on. It is a miracle that we did not have an accident on that early peaceful Sunday morning. My praise and thank you went to Almighty God.

We need to take a closer look at many concerns. These can be the concerns that can help us to maneuver through life with fewer headaches, heartaches, and pain as we drive on the roadways. It is sad but true that many individuals think, while driving, *It is all about me. I must be first at all times. I have to be in front of you.*

I will turn at a stop sign without stopping. This is selfish in the meanest way possible.

I been driving for more than forty-five years, and I have gained some wisdom in driving that I want to share:

1. Driving is a precious gift; be courteous to other drivers while one is doing it.
2. Driving is not all about you. You do not have to be first at all times. You do not have to be first at the traffic light. And you do not have to be first to take off from the traffic light. You do have to be courteous to other drivers at all times; the opposite of courtesy is being selfish.
3. Always be patient when stopped at a traffic light. Slow down as you approach the light.
4. Never, ever tailgate. It is truly a hazardous to one's health. It can cause multiple accidents, and many vehicles will be out of service for a while.

    This is wisdom speaking from a divine perspective. When people apply these steps in driving, a change will come to the drivers in a positive way. There will be less stress in driving when you use these steps. The power to stay focused when driving can be challenging at times. This can come from being too tired to drive. The wisest thing to do in this instance is to pull over at a rest stop and take a nap or get some coffee.
5. Be sure the vehicle you are driving has working headlights and taillights. Please use them at all times but especially in the dark, rain, fog, and early mornings hours. Embrace safety first before starting the engine in any vehicle.
6. Use the signal light when making a turn or changing of lanes. Be sure to drive on low beam when approaching oncoming traffic. This will allow the driver facing the oncoming headlights to have less of a challenge in seeing where he or she is driving. These are rules to drive by and stay safe out there.

7. Be sure to drive defensively at all times. Stay alert and be courteous to all drivers. Also, driving offensively can be positive in a special way to yourself and others. The highways and freeways are roads we have to travel to get from point A to point Z. Let's come together and share the road in love toward our fellow humans.

CHAPTER 40

◆

Entrepreneurship: Watch, Wait, Work

The following in-an-instant moment relates to my first job, my first business opportunity. My oldest sister, Dorothy, also called Dot, gave me the chance to apply myself in this position. She didn't pressure me to do what I needed to do in order to be successful. After all, I was capable and willing to prove that I was worthy of this remarkable opportunity. This position was not the greatest job, but it was a way for me to start making an honest living and provide for myself at an early age. I praise God for giving me a blessed mindset of wanting to do this at an early age.

Today's title for my job would be yardman or groundskeeper. I would rake the front yard of fallen leaves in the fall and winter. Then, when spring and summer arrived, I would cut the grass every week or so. Afterwards, Dot paid me several dollars for my efforts. This allowed me to have some spending money to purchase the things I desired. I was only nine or ten years old at the time, but I saw myself as a businessman one day. I had the drive, determination, ambition, and vision within to do so.

I would like to share the three W's. They are the building blocks for a solid foundation to establish an honest business relationship with the public. They are *watch, wait, and work.*

Watch: There are numerous opportunities all around us to start a business. You only need to open your eyes to see the needs of the people. It may or may not be an ideal job for you, but it can be an honest, paying opportunity for your service. To discover the needs of the people, you must be a great listener to hear what people are saying.

Wait: You must wait in order to be prepared for the right opportunity and to prove yourself worthy of such a job and responsibility. What should you do as you wait for the right opportunity? Take the waiting period to educate yourself on the service you are willing to offer to potential clients. Hone in to shape, sharpen, and create the best of service in the field that you can offer to your clients. Have a cheerful outlook; that will better prepare you for the business opportunity whenever it presents itself. Be positive in every way. There is power when you think and feel positive about your new venture.

Work: This is the crucial aspect of any business. You must work to do your absolute best so you can be effective and efficient every day, as if it's the first day of business. The hours may be exceptionally long and chaotic, but don't admit defeat. You must press on and keep looking up to where your help, knowledge, and wisdom came from. Your help comes from God of Creation. He knows your purpose in life before you were born.

When you apply the three W's, there is a greater chance that the business will survive in the start-up season to grow and be the business that God has predestined for you to be steward over.

◆ ◆ ◆

Even though I was working for Dot, I saw another opportunity for another service to offer another one of my siblings. From an early age, I loved to iron my clothes—so much so that one of my older brothers gave me the opportunity to offer my services to him. He paid me for ironing his clothes.

Several years later, this led me to another opportunity—to start my business, Isaiah Art Design, which I established in 1992.[2] My desire is to grow it to a greater level as I near my retirement, by the grace and mercy of God, in Christ Jesus's name, amen.

I hope my testimonies and stories will be building blocks for humankind and will be the productive tool to help you to better fulfill your purpose in society. It is such a unique gift to embrace for the rest of one's life on earth.

We are a blessed nation and have so much to give to others. Let us set aside our differences. Let us disagree but not be disagreeable. That opens the door of opportunity to display hate instead of love toward others. This is the land of the free, where we are free by choice to show love to others. Please do not allow the enemy to use and divide us from what is woven in our DNA in the great U.S.A.

It is a personal choice for everyone, to live and do right toward others. Think on these things and make them one of your highest aims. The end result will be a powerful gain in your life.

Eternity still waits for all to be on board with a higher plain on higher ground, God, help us to plant our feet in eternity like that.

---

[2] You can visit my website at designinspirational.com, or you can google "Isaiah Art."

Printed in the United States
by Baker & Taylor Publisher Services